Lecture Notes in Comput

2

Edited by G. Goos, J. Hartmanis and

Advisory Board: W. Brauer D. Gries J. Stoer

Springer

Berlin
Heidelberg
New York
Barcelona
Budapest
Hong Kong
London
Milan
Paris
Santa Clara
Singapore
Tokyo

Patrice Godefroid

Partial-Order Methods for the Verification of Concurrent Systems

An Approach to the State-Explosion Problem

Springer

Series Editors

Gerhard Goos
Universität Karlsruhe
Vincenz-Priessnitz-Straße 3, D-76128 Karlsruhe, Germany

Juris Hartmanis
Department of Computer Science, Cornell University
4130 Upson Hall, Ithaca, NY 14853, USA

Jan van Leeuwen
Department of Computer Science,Utrecht University
Padualaan 14, 3584 CH Utrecht, The Netherlands

Author

Patrice Godefroid
AT&T Bell Laboratories
1000 E. Warrenville Road, Naperville, IL 60566-7013, USA

Cataloging-in-Publication data applied for

Die Deutsche Bibliothek - CIP-Einheitsaufnahme

Godefroid, Patrice:
Partial order methods for the verification of concurrent
systems : an approach to the state explosion problem / Patrice
Godefroid. - Berlin ; Heidelberg ; New York ; Barcelona ;
Budapest ; Hong Kong ; London ; Milan ; Paris ; Santa Clara ;
Singapore ; Tokyo : Springer, 1996
  (Lecture notes in computer science ; 1032)
  ISBN 3-540-60761-7
NE: GT

CR Subject Classification (1991): F.3.1, D.2.4, C.2.2, F.1.2, D.2.4

ISBN 3-540-60761-7 Springer-Verlag Berlin Heidelberg New York

© Springer-Verlag Berlin Heidelberg 1996
Printed in Germany

Typesetting: Camera-ready by author
SPIN 10512431   06/3142 – 5 4 3 2 1 0   Printed on acid-free paper

Foreword

For many years, research on verification dealt almost exclusively with semantic and logical issues. A typical thesis on the subject would consider some delicate programming feature and show how a proof system could be extended to handle this feature. A completeness proof added some theoretical meat, and a laboriously worked out toy example showed that it was, at least in principle, possible to use the new proof system. With few exceptions, little thought was given to implementing the verification approach and making it painlessly usable by the typical practicing software developer.

Although this thesis deals with verification, it is far from following the pattern outlined above. Indeed, rather than being about a logical system for verification, it is about *algorithms* for verification. Its starting point is the simple technique of state-space exploration, which as such, or elaborated into model checking, is attracting growing attention for the verification of concurrent systems. Patrice Godefroid addresses a main limiting factor of this approach: the explosion of the number of states due to the modeling of concurrency by interleaving. Noticing that, as indicated by partial-order semantics for concurrency, this limiting factor is not inherent, he proceeds to develop a family of algorithms that make it possible to avoid it. Furthermore, these algorithms have been implemented, and experiments show that they can work very well in practice.

The general pattern of this thesis is thus to turn logical and semantic ideas into exploitable algorithms. It is part of the trend that views verification as a computer-aided (and as algorithmic as possible) activity, not as a paper and pencil one. After all, if software engineers are going to check their designs, they need, as all other engineers, computer support to do so.

There is much valuable information in this thesis. The verification systems builder will find a guide to implementing partial-order state space exploration techniques. The user of verification systems will gain a knowledge of how these methods work, and of why they are entirely reliable. The computer scientist will enjoy the beauty of clear algorithms crystallizing from the simple semantic concept of independent transitions.

Pierre Wolper

Preface

State-space exploration techniques are increasingly being used for debugging and proving correct finite-state concurrent reactive systems. The reason for this success is mainly the simplicity of these techniques. Indeed, they are easy to understand, easy to implement, and, last but not least, easy to use: they are fully automatic. Moreover, the range of properties that they can verify has been substantially broadened thanks to the development of model-checking methods for various temporal logics.

The main limit of state-space exploration verification techniques is the often excessive size of the state space, due, among other causes, to the modeling of concurrency by interleaving. However, exploring *all* interleavings of concurrent events is not a priori necessary for verification: interleavings corresponding to the same concurrent execution contain related information. One can thus hope to be able to verify properties of a concurrent system without exploring all interleavings of its concurrent executions. This work presents a collection of methods, called *partial-order methods*, that make this possible.

The intuition behind partial-order methods is that concurrent executions are really partial orders and that concurrent events should be left unordered since the order of their occurrence is irrelevant. However, rather than choosing to work with direct representations of partial orders, the methods we develop keep to an interleaving representation of partial orders, but attempt to limit the expansion of each partial-order computation to just *one* of its interleavings, instead of all of them. More precisely, given a property, partial-order methods explore only a reduced part of the global state-space that is sufficient for checking the given property. In this work, three types of properties are considered: absence of deadlocks, safety properties, and properties expressed by linear-time temporal-logic formulas.

The techniques and algorithms we describe have been implemented in an add-on package for the protocol verification system SPIN. This *Partial-Order Package* has been tested on numerous examples, including several industrial-size communication protocols. When the coupling between the processes is very tight, partial-order methods yield no reduction, and the partial-order search becomes equivalent to a classical exhaustive search. When the coupling between the processes is very loose, the reduction is very impressive: in some cases, the number of states that need to be visited for verification can be reduced from exponential to polynomial in the size of the system description (code). For most realistic examples, partial-order methods provide a

4

significant reduction of the memory and time requirements needed to verify protocols.

This monograph is a revised version of my PhD thesis, submitted in 1994 to the University of Liège. This work would not have been possible without the technical and moral support of my thesis advisor, Pierre Wolper. He introduced me to the field of verification, and opened doors for me in the research community. His enthusiastic supervision has been a continuous source of encouragement to me. I consider myself fortunate that I had access to his valuable guidance.

I am grateful to the other members of my reading committee, Professors Raymond Devillers, Pascal Gribomont, Amir Pnueli, Daniel Ribbens, Joseph Sifakis, and Antti Valmari, for their very careful review of this work.

It has been a great pleasure for me to work closely with Didier Pirottin during these last three years. I am thankful to Didier for numerous insightful discussions, and for his help in implementing algorithms presented in this work.

I wish to thank Gerard Holzmann for freely sharing his considerable experience in validating communication protocols. I learned how to build verification tools mainly from his work and from discussions with him. He provided me with many challenging examples of communication protocols, which have been (and still are) a very good source of inspiration to me. He also made possible an exciting visit to AT&T Bell Laboratories during the summer of 1992.

I have had the opportunity to discuss my research with many scientists at various conferences and seminars. I thank all of them for being helpful and encouraging. I am particularly grateful to Mark Drummond, Pascal Gribomont, Froduald Kabanza, Doron Peled, and Antti Valmari for very fruitful discussions. Special thanks also go to Bernard Boigelot, Philippe Lejoly, and Luc Moreau for reading and commenting on an early version of this text, and to Gerald Luettgen and Bernhard Steffen for detailed comments and suggestions.

This work was financially supported by the European Community ESPRIT projects SPEC (3096) and REACT (6021), and by the Belgian Incentive Program "Information Technology – Computer Science of the Future", initiated by the Belgian State – Prime Minister's Service – Science Policy Office, which I gratefully acknowledge. I thank AT&T Bell Laboratories for the additional time which made it possible for me to complete this revision of my thesis.

Last but not least, I wish to thank my parents for their constant moral support, and Anne-Christine for her love, for sharing ups and downs, and for reminding me, when necessary, that computer science is not the most important thing in life.

Contents

List of Figures

Chapter 1

Introduction

1.1 Background and Motivation

Concurrent systems are systems composed of elements that can operate concurrently and communicate with each other. Each component can be viewed as a *reactive system*, i.e., a system that continuously interacts with its environment. The environment of one component is formed by the other components of the concurrent system, which is hence assumed to be closed. (This implies that, in case of a single "open" reactive system, a model of the environment in which this system operates has to be represented by other component(s) of the concurrent system, in order to close the system.) The behavior of a reactive system is defined by its ongoing behavior over time. This is quite unlike the traditional "transformational" view of programs where the functional relationship between the input state and the output state defines the meaning of a program. Indeed, reactive systems are not dedicated to the transformation of data (like traditional programs), but rather to the control of processes. There are many examples of such concurrent reactive systems: computer networks, asynchronous circuits, operating systems, and various forms of plant-controller systems, such as telephone switches, flight-control systems, manufacturing-plant controllers, etc.

Concurrent reactive systems are notably difficult to design. Indeed, such systems can usually exhibit an extremely large number of different behaviors. This is due to the combinatorial explosion resulting from all possible interactions between the different concurrent components of the system, and the many possible race conditions that may arise between them. This situation makes the development of concurrent reactive systems an extremely delicate task. Testing is also of very limited help since test coverage is bound to be only a minute fraction of the possible behaviors of the system. This situation is all the more alarming since reactive systems are increasingly being used to control safety-critical devices (e.g., flight-control systems) or economically-crucial systems (e.g., telephone switches).

Verification provides the mean to ensure the correctness of the design of concurrent reactive systems. Verification means checking that a system description conforms to its expected properties. These properties can range from several forms of consistency to complex correctness requirements specified, for instance, in a logical language. Verification is thus the tool that enables the designer to be confident that the formal description of the system he/she has obtained does indeed satisfy the problem requirements.

Four elements are necessary to define a *verification framework*:

- a representation of the system,

- a representation of the property to be checked,

- a conformation criterion according to which the representations of the system and of the property are compared, and

- a method (preferably an automatic algorithm) for performing this comparison.

Note that "verify" means to (mathematically) *prove* that a system meets its correctness requirements. We specifically do not mean testing (unless it is exhaustive) or any other method that ensures that the system is "probably" correct. In order to prove that a system conforms to a property, *all possible behaviors* of the system have to be checked to determine if all of them are compatible with the given property.

State-space exploration is one of the most successful strategies for analyzing and verifying finite-state concurrent reactive systems. It consists in exploring a global state graph representing the combined behavior of all concurrent components in the system. This is done by recursively exploring all successor states of all states encountered during the exploration, starting from a given initial state, by executing all enabled transitions in each state. The state graph that is explored is called the *state space* of the system. If the state space is finite, it can be explored completely.

Many different types of properties of a system can be checked by exploring its state space: deadlocks, dead code, violations of user-specified assertions, etc. Moreover, the range of properties that state-space exploration techniques can verify has been substantially broadened during the last decade thanks to the development of model-checking methods for various temporal logics (e.g., [CES86, LP85, QS81, VW86]).

Verification by state-space exploration has been studied by many researchers (cf. [Liu89, Rud87]). The simplicity of the strategy lends itself to easy, and thus efficient, implementations. Moreover, verification by state-space exploration is fully automatic: no intervention of the designer is required. This is a crucial feature for a verification technique to be used in industry. Indeed, systems are often (read always) developed under time pressure, and verification steps that would be too much time consuming for the designer are therefore not realistic.

All these reasons explain why many present verification tools follow this paradigm. Examples of such tools are CAESAR[FGM+92], COSPAN[HK90], MURPHI[DDHY92], SPIN [Hol91], among others. These tools differ by the formal description languages they use for representing systems and properties, and by the conformation criterion according to which these representations are compared. But all of them are based on state-space exploration algorithms, in one form or another, for performing the verification itself.

As tools are being developed, the effectiveness of state-space exploration techniques for debugging and proving correct concurrent reactive systems is increasingly becoming established. The number of "success stories" about applying these techniques to industrial-size systems keeps growing (e.g., see [Rud92]). Several very complex examples of concurrent systems have been analyzed and verified using state-space exploration techniques. In many cases, these techniques were able to reveal quite subtle design errors.

The main limit of state-space exploration verification techniques is the often excessive size of the state space. Owing to simple combinatorics, this size can be exponential in the size of the description of the system being analyzed. This exponential growth is known as the *state-explosion problem.*

The state-explosion problem is due, among other causes, to the modeling of concurrency by interleaving, or, more accurately, to the exploration of all possible interleavings of concurrent events. For instance, the execution of n concurrent events is investigated by exploring all $n!$ interleavings of these events.

In this work, we develop an original approach for applying verification by state-space exploration without incurring most of the cost of modeling concurrency by interleaving.

1.2   Partial-Order Methods

We show that exploring *all* interleavings of concurrent events is not a priori necessary for verification: interleavings corresponding to the same concurrent execution contain related information. One can thus hope to be able to verify properties of a concurrent system without exploring all interleavings of its concurrent executions. This work presents a collection of methods, called *partial-order methods*, that make this possible.

The intuition behind partial-order methods is that concurrent executions are really partial orders and that expanding such a partial order into the set of *all* its interleavings is an inefficient way of analyzing concurrent executions. Instead, concurrent events should be left unordered since the order of their occurrence is irrelevant. Hence the name "partial-order methods". However, rather than choosing to work with direct representations of partial orders, the methods we develop keep to an interleaving representation of partial orders, but attempt to limit the expansion of each partial-order computation to just *one* of its interleavings, instead of all of them.

Precisely, given a property, partial-order methods explore only a reduced part of the global state space that is provably sufficient to check the given property. The difference between the reduced and the global state spaces is that all interleavings of concurrent events are not systematically represented in the reduced one. We will see later that which interleavings are required to be preserved may depend on the property to be checked.

The specification of the algorithms we develop is that they have to *verify* a given property of a finite-state concurrent system while exploring as small a fraction as possible of its state space. In this work, we present algorithms for exploring reduced state spaces for the verification of three types of properties: absence of deadlocks, safety properties, and linear-time temporal-logic formulas. These types of properties are considered separately because checking more elaborate properties requires the preservation of more information in the reduced state space, i.e, the exploration of more states and transitions. It is therefore worth developing specific algorithms for the verification of standard types of properties, and then using the appropriate algorithm for each property in order to maximize the amount of reduction that can be obtained in practice.

It must be noted that, though the partial-order methods we develop are inspired by partial-order semantics (especially by Mazurkiewicz's traces [Maz86]), these methods do not comply with any specific partial-order semantics. Indeed, the only requirement is that the modified concurrent composition computes enough interleavings to make checking the desired property possible. Not all concurrent executions need be represented if the verification does not require it and, conversely, a given concurrent execution can be represented by several redundant interleavings. The prime concern is to check the desired property as efficiently as possible.

1.3 Related Work

It has been recognized for some time that concurrency and nondeterminism are not the same thing. This observation has inspired a fairly large body of work on so-called "partial-order models" of concurrency (cf. [Lam78, Maz86, Pra86, Win86]). Work in this area studies various semantics for concurrency, and compares their properties. In this work, we take a more pragmatic point of view towards partial-order models: our goal is to develop verification methods for concurrent finite-state systems that avoid the part of the combinatorial explosion due to the modeling of concurrency by interleaving. Our approach yields results identical to those of methods based on classical interleaving semantics, it just avoids most of the associated combinatorial explosion. It is also quite orthogonal to the verification of properties expressed in partial-order temporal logics (cf. [PW84, KP86, KP87, Pen88, Pen90]). Indeed, these logics are designed to be semantically more expressive. We are "only" more efficient.

Several approximate methods based on simple heuristics have been proposed to restrict the number of interleavings that are explored [GH85, Wes86, Hol87]. These heuristics carry with them the risk of incomplete verification results, i.e., they can detect errors but cannot prove the absence of errors. In contrast, the partial-order methods we develop in this work reduce the number of interleavings that must be inspected in a completely reliable manner, provably without the risk of any incompleteness in the verification results.

The closest work to the one presented here is certainly that of Valmari [Val91], which extends previous work done by Overman [Ove81]. Indeed, Valmari has developed an approach (based on "stubborn sets") for generating reduced state spaces that can be used for checking properties of concurrent systems whithout considering all interleavings of concurrent events. Despite this general similarity with our approach, there are many differences that distinguish Valmari's work from ours. These important technical differences will be pointed out during the presentation of this work. Note, as a first notable difference, that Valmari does not rely on any partial-order semantics to justify and prove the correctness of his algorithms. This makes the presentation of the stubborn set method (see [Val91]) less modular and, we believe, less intuitive than the style of presentation using partial-order semantics (precisely Mazurkiewicz's traces) adopted in this work. This is of course a subjective point of view. However, this issue has implications that go beyond a simple question of presentation. Indeed, using partial orders and a notion of (in)dependency as done in this work, we were able, among other things, to generalize and improve the stubborn set method, as will be presented in Chapter 4. This is a more solid argument in favor of our approach to the problem. In any case, our partial-order approach indubitably brings a new perspective on Valmari's stubborn set theory.

Strategies for proving properties of concurrent systems without considering all possible interleavings of their concurrent actions have been proposed in [AFdR80, EF82, Pnu85, SdR89, KP92b, JZ93]. These proof methods are applied in the context of an inference system, in which the correctness of a system is established by proving assertions about its components. This approach to verification has the advantage of not being restricted to finite-state systems. On the other hand, it requires proofs that are manual. Even with the help of a theorem prover, carrying out proofs with a theorem prover is far from fully automatic since most steps of the proof require inventive interventions from the user. In contrast, the focus of this work is purely on algorithmic issues, since we discuss fully-automatic state-space exploration techniques.

The idea that the cost of modeling concurrency by interleaving can be avoided in finite-state verification also appeared in [JK90, PL90, McM92, Esp94]. In [JK90], the problem of finding an "optimal" reduced state space with just enough transitions and states to preserve Mazurkiewicz's trace semantics is addressed. In [PL90], a method that relies on a pomset grammar description of the system is introduced. Also, in [McM92, Esp94], one finds a verification method that works by unfolding a Petri net description of a concurrent system into a finite acyclic structure. These methods are quite different from those developed in this work. Note that none of these other methods have been widely experimented on a large set of realistic examples, as it has been the case for the methods presented here (see Chapter 8).

Other approaches to the state-explosion problem have been proposed. By using (ordered) *Binary Decision Diagrams* (BDDs) [Bry92] to represent *"symbolically"* transition systems and sets of reachable states, it is possible to explore very large regular state spaces (e.g., [BCM+90, McM93]). Symbolic verification will be further discussed in Chapter 8. In *compositional verification*, local properties of components in the system are checked, and then used to prove the correctness of the overall system (e.g., [CLM89, GS90, Lon93]). Compositionality is also one of the main motivations behind the work on *process algebras* (e.g., [Mil80, BK85, Hoa85, Hen88]). With *ab-*

straction methods, models of systems are simplified by hiding details (e.g., [CC77, Dil89, Kur89, CGL92, GL93]). Compositional and abstraction methods are part of a divide-and-conquer strategy for verification: they are used to reduce a complex verification problem into several, hopefully more manageable, sub-problems. Successful use of these approaches requires some knowledge from the user of how parts of the system contribute to satisfying the property to be checked. These approaches are essentially orthogonal to the partial-order methods we consider in this work, and are complementary to them. In general, the larger the state space that can be searched automatically, the less the need for abstraction and compositionality. Since verification is an active area of research at the time of this writing, we refer the reader to the journals and the proceedings of the conferences cited in the bibliography given at the end of the document for further information on other work on this topic.

The key contributions of the material presented in this work already appeared in a series of papers [God90, GW91a, GW91b, GHP92, HGP92, GP93, GW93, WG93, GW94]. The monograph presents most of the results published in these papers in a unified framework, and relates them with each other. It also extends several of these results. References to preliminary published versions are included in the presentation of the following chapters.

1.4 Organization of this Work

In Chapter 2, we introduce a simple model for representing concurrent systems, and define its semantics. Then, we motivate the choice of this model, and compare it to other existing models and formalisms.

In Chapter 3, we show that exploring all possible interleavings of all possible "independent" transitions of a system is not necessary for verification. We precisely define the notion of independency, and discuss how to detect independency between transitions in concurrent systems. Interleavings of independent transitions are related by the notion of Mazurkiewicz's trace. The algorithms developed in this work take advantage of the independency between transitions to avoid exploring all their interleavings, and thus to avoid exploring parts of the state space. Such a partial exploration of the state space is called a selective search.

In Chapter 4, a first technique for determining the transitions that need to be explored in a selective search, called the persistent set technique, is presented. This technique actually corresponds to a whole family of existing algorithms, which are presented, discussed, and compared with each other. Then, a new algorithm that generalizes and improves the previous ones in a sense that will be given later is described.

In Chapter 5, another technique for selecting transitions to be explored in a selective search, called the sleep set technique, is introduced. Sleep sets are shown to be compatible with persistent sets, and their properties are studied.

In Chapter 6, the persistent set and sleep set techniques, used for deadlock detection in Chapters 4 and 5, are extended in order to make possible the verification of arbitrary safety properties. Trace automata are introduced to justify the correctness of this extension.

In Chapter 7, we address the model-checking problem for linear-time temporal-logic. We point out the key problems underlying the verification of liveness properties using partial-order methods, and compare the solutions that have been proposed for solving these problems. We also show how the proposed techniques complement each other.

In Chapter 8, results of experiments on various examples using the algorithms that have been developed in this work are presented. These algorithms have been implemented in an add-on package for the protocol verification system SPIN. This partial-order package is briefly described, and instructions for obtaining a copy of it by anonymous ftp are given. The complementarity between partial-order methods and state-space caching is also pointed out. The practical contributions of partial-order methods are finally discussed.

In Chapter 9, a summary of this work is presented together with some areas for further study.

Chapter 2

Concurrent Systems and Semantics

In this chapter, we introduce a simple representation for modeling concurrent systems, and define its semantics. Then, we motivate the choice of this model, and compare it to other existing models and formalisms.

2.1 Representing Concurrent Systems

Concurrent systems are composed of different components, called processes, that can act in parallel and interact with each other. In this work, we will assume that processes are *finite-state*, i.e., that the number of states that they can reach is finite. We will also assume that processes can synchronize by executing together joint transitions (rendezvous), and communicate by performing operations on shared objects. Formally, our model for representing concurrent systems is the following.

A *labeled formal concurrent system* (LFCS), or *system* for short, is a tuple $(\mathcal{P}, \mathcal{O}, \mathcal{T}, \nu, s_0)$, where

- $\mathcal{P}$ is a finite set of n *processes*,

- $\mathcal{O}$ is a finite set of m *objects*,

- $\mathcal{T}$ is a finite set of *transitions*,

- $\nu : \mathcal{T} \mapsto \Sigma$ is a *labeling function* that associates a label, also called an *action*, taken from an alphabet Σ with each transition of $\mathcal{T}$, and

- s_0 is the *initial state* of the system.

Each *process* $P_i \in \mathcal{P}$ is a finite nonempty set of *local states*, or *control points*. Processes are pairwise disjoint.

Processes can access a finite set of objects. An object O is characterized by a pair (V, OP), where V is the set of all possible values for the object (its domain), and OP is the set of *operations* that can be performed on the object. Each operation $op_i \in OP$ is a (possibly partial) function $IN_i \times V \rightarrow OUT_i \times V$, where IN_i and OUT_i represent respectively the set of possible inputs and outputs of the operation. The notation $op_i(in, v) \rightarrow (out, v')$ denotes the fact that the execution of the operation $op_i \in OP$ with input value $in \in IN_i$ while the value of the object is v yields an output value $out \in OUT_i$ and changes the value of the object to v'. For operations op_i that do not take an input (resp. do not return an output), the set IN_i (resp. OUT_i) degenerates to a singleton, and we denote its unique meaningless value by "–".

Example 2.1 Consider an object "boolean variable" whose domain V is the set $\{0, 1\}$. We define two operations on this object.

- A *Read* operation for which the set IN is $\{-\}$, and the set OUT is $\{0, 1\}$. A *Read* operation is always defined, and its effect is defined by $Read(-, v) \rightarrow (v, v)$, for all $v \in \{0, 1\}$.

- A *Write* operation for which the set IN is $\{0, 1\}$, and the set OUT is $\{-\}$. A *Write* operation is always defined, and its effect is defined by $Write(v', v) \rightarrow (-, v')$, for all $v, v' \in \{0, 1\}$.

∎

A *global state* s, or simply a *state*, of a system is an element of the set $S = P_1 \times \ldots \times P_n \times V_1 \times \ldots \times V_m$. A state $s = (s(1), s(2), \ldots, s(n), v(1), v(2), \ldots, v(m))$ assigns to each process P_i a local state $s(i) \in P_i$ of this process (this can be viewed as the formal counterpart of the notion of "program counter" for a physical process), and associates a value $v(j) \in V_j$ with each object O_j. The initial state s_0 is an element of S. In what follows, we write $l \in s$ to mean $\exists i, 1 \leq i \leq n$ such that $l = s(i)$, i.e., for notational convenience we allow ourselves to view the state s as a set rather than as a vector.

A transition $t \in T$ is a tuple (L, G, C, L'). Both L and L' are *partial control states*, i.e., nonempty subsets of $\cup_{i=1}^{n} P_i$ such that for each $1 \leq i \leq n$, $|L \cap P_i| = |L' \cap P_i| \leq 1$.

The sets L and L' are respectively called the *preset* and *postset* of the transition t. In the sequel, $pre(t)$ denotes the preset of the transition t, while $post(t)$ denotes the postset of the transition t. The processes P_i's that participate in a transition t, i.e., the processes P_i's such that $|L \cap P_i| = |L' \cap P_i| = 1$, are said to be *active* for this transition. The set of processes that are active for a transition t is denoted by $active(t)$. The *guard* G of the transition is a conjunction of conditions c_j. Conditions c_j in G can test the current value of objects by using operations on these objects that do not modify their value. The *command* C of the transition is a function from $V_1 \times \ldots \times V_m$ to $V_1 \times \ldots \times V_m$ defined by a sequential composition of operations on objects, with the restriction that an operation that modifies the value of an object O_j cannot be followed by any other operation on O_j in the remainder of the sequence of operations defining the command.

For instance, if x and y are two objects of type "boolean variable" as defined in Example 2.1, "$x := y$" denotes a command that performs a *Read* operation on object y, and then performs a *Write* operation on object x with the output value returned by the *Read* operation. If x is $v(k)$ and y is $v(l)$, the function defined by the command $x := y$ is the function f from $V_1 \times \ldots \times V_m$ to $V_1 \times \ldots \times V_m$ such that $f((v(1), v(2), \ldots, v(m))) = (v'(1), v'(2), \ldots, v'(m))$ where $v'(i) = v(i)$, $i \neq k$, and $v'(k) = v(l)$.

We assume that, for each operation op that appears in the command C of a transition, if op is not defined for all inputs and all values of the object, there is a condition c_j (expressed by using operations on the object and predicates on its domain and the domain of its inputs and outputs) in the guard G of the transition such that op is defined iff c_j is true. Operations that appear either in the guard G or in the command C of a transition are said *to be used by* this transition. The set of operations that are used by a transition t is denoted by $used(t)$. An object is said *to be accessed by* a transition if the transition uses an operation on the object.

A transition $t = (L, G, C, L')$ is *enabled* in a state s iff $L \subseteq s$ and G is true in s. If t is not enabled in s, t is said to be *disabled* in state s. A transition t that is enabled in a state $s = (s(1), s(2), \ldots, s(n), v(1), v(2), \ldots, v(m))$ can be *executed*. After the execution of t, the system reaches a state $s' = (s'(1), s'(2), \ldots, s'(n), v'(1), v'(2), \ldots, v'(m))$ such that:

- $\{s'(1), s'(2), \ldots, s'(n)\} = (\{s(1), s(2), \ldots, s(n)\} \setminus L) \cup L'$; and

- the command C maps $(v(1), v(2), \ldots, v(m))$ to $(v'(1), v'(2), \ldots, v'(m))$.

State s' is called the *successor* of s by t. We write $s \xrightarrow{t} s'$ to mean that the transition

t leads from the state s to the state s', while $s \overset{w}{\Rightarrow} s'$ means that the finite sequence of transitions w leads from s to s'. If $s \overset{w}{\Rightarrow} s'$, s' is said to be *reachable* from s.

Note 2.2 Transitions, as well as operations on objects, are *deterministic*: the execution of a transition t in a state s leads to a *unique* successor state. This is not a restriction since "nondeterministic transitions" can always be modeled by a set of deterministic transitions with non mutually exclusive guards. ■

2.2 Semantics

A concurrent system as defined here is a closed system: from its initial state, it can evolve and change its state by executing enabled transitions. Therefore, a very natural way to describe the possible *behaviors* of such a system is to consider its set of reachable global states and the transitions that are possible between these.

More specifically, the joint *global* behavior of all processes P_i in a LFCS can be represented by an automaton $A_G = (\Sigma, S, \Delta, s_0)$ where

- Σ is the alphabet of actions of the LFCS,

- S is the set of states of the LFCS,

- $\Delta \subseteq S \times \Sigma \times S$ is the *transition relation* defined as follows:

$$(s, a, s') \in \Delta \text{ iff } \exists t \in \mathcal{T} : s \overset{t}{\rightarrow} s' \wedge a = \nu(t),$$

- s_0 is the initial state of the LFCS.

A transition of Δ corresponds to the execution of a single transition $t \in \mathcal{T}$ of the system, and is labeled by $\nu(t)$. To avoid any confusion with the transitions of $\mathcal{T}$, transitions of Δ will be referred to as *global transitions*, while transitions of $\mathcal{T}$ will be referred to as *transitions*.

It is natural to restrict A_G to its states and transitions that are reachable from s_0, since the other states and transitions play no role in the behavior of the system. In what follows, a "state in A_G" denotes a state that is reachable from the initial state s_0. A_G is called the global state graph or *global state space* of the system.

Unless otherwise specified, we will assume that the domain of all objects is finite. This implies that the size of A_G is finite.

```
1    Initialize:Stack is empty; H is empty;
2              push (s₀) onto Stack;
3    Loop: while Stack ≠ ∅ do {
4              pop (s) from Stack;
5              if s is NOT already in H then {
6                enter s in H;
7                T = enabled(s);
8                for all t in T do {
9                  s' = succ(s) after t; /* execution of t */
10                 push (s') onto Stack;
11                 }
12               }
13             }
```

Figure 2.1: Classical search

In practice, A_G can be computed by performing a search of all the states that are reachable from the initial state s_0. An algorithm for performing such a search is shown in Figure 2.1. This algorithm recursively explores all successor states of all states encountered during the search, starting from the initial state, by executing all enabled transitions in each state (line 7–8). The main data structures used are a *Stack* to store the states whose successors still have to be explored, and a hash table H to store all the states that have already been visited during the search. The set of all transitions that are enabled in a state s is denoted by *enabled(s)*. The state reached from a state s after the execution of a transition t is denoted "succ(s) after t". It is easy to prove that all the states of A_G, i.e., all the states that are reachable from s_0, are visited during the search performed by the algorithm of Figure 2.1 [AHU74].

For the time being, let us define the set of possible *behaviors* of a system as the set of all possible *finite* sequences of labels (actions) that the system can execute from its initial state. (Infinite sequences will be considered later in Chapter 7.) Formally, a finite sequence (word) $w = a_1 a_2 \ldots a_n$ of actions in Σ is *accepted* by A_G if there is a sequence of states $\sigma = s_0 \ldots s_n$ such that s_0 is the initial state of A_G and, for all $1 \leq i \leq n$, $(s_{i-1}, a_i, s_i) \in \Delta$. We call such a sequence σ a *computation* of A_G on w. The set of words accepted by A_G is called the *language accepted by A_G*. With our definition, this language is prefix closed.

2.3   Example

As an example of concurrent system, consider the well-known dining-philosophers problem, with two philosophers. This system can be modeled by the following LFCS.

- $\mathcal{P} = \{A, B\}$, where $A = \{a_0, a_1, a_2, a_3\}$ and $B = \{b_0, b_1, b_2, b_3\}$ (the system is composed of two processes A and B; each process models one philosopher);

- $\mathcal{O} = \{f_1, f_2\}$, where f_1 and f_2 are two objects of type "boolean variable" as defined in Example 2.1 (f_1 and f_2 model two forks that can be accessed by philosophers A and B);

- $\mathcal{T} = \{t_1^A, t_2^A, t_3^A, t_4^A, t_1^B, t_2^B, t_3^B, t_4^B\}$, where

$$
\begin{array}{llll}
t_1^A = (a_0, f_1 = 0, f_1 := 1, a_1), & t_1^B = (b_0, f_2 = 0, f_2 := 1, b_1), & \text{(take left fork)} \\
t_2^A = (a_1, f_2 = 0, f_2 := 1, a_2), & t_2^B = (b_1, f_1 = 0, f_1 := 1, b_2), & \text{(take right fork)} \\
t_3^A = (a_2, true, f_1 := 0, a_3), & t_3^B = (b_2, true, f_2 := 0, b_3), & \text{(release left fork)} \\
t_4^A = (a_3, true, f_2 := 0, a_0), & t_4^B = (b_3, true, f_1 := 0, b_0). & \text{(release right fork)}
\end{array}
$$

- $\nu : \mathcal{T} \mapsto \Sigma$ is the identity function from $\mathcal{T}$ to itself;

- $s_0 = (a_0, b_0, 0, 0) \in A \times B \times V_{f_1} \times V_{f_2}$ (initially, A is in state a_0, B is in state b_0, and the two forks are released).

Forks are modeled by boolean variables f_i. When f_i is equal to 0, fork f_i is ready to be taken by any philosopher. When f_i is equal to 1, fork f_i is already taken by a philosopher, and cannot be taken by the other. Consider philosopher A. From its initial local control state a_0, A can try to take fork f_1: this is modeled by transition t_1^A where process A tests in its guard if fork f_1 is available (it tests if f_1 is equal to 0), and then takes it if it is available by executing $f_1 := 1$ (it sets the value of f_1 to 1). Then, process A can try to take fork f_2 in a similar way by trying to execute transition t_2^A. When A has taken both its left and right forks, i.e., when it reaches its local state a_2, it can eat. Then, it releases its left fork (transition t_3^A) and next its right fork (transition t_4^A), and goes back to its initial (thinking) state. Process B proceeds in a similar way.

The global state space A_G of the two-dining-philosophers system is shown in Figure 2.2. It contains 8 states and 10 transitions.

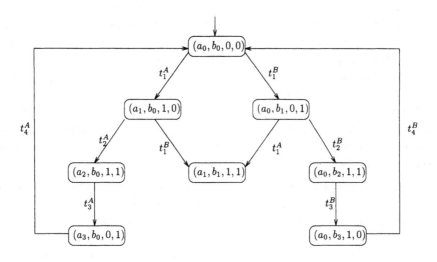

Figure 2.2: Global state space for the two-dining-philosophers system

2.4 Discussion

Why did we choose to represent concurrent systems by labeled formal concurrent systems (LFCS) as defined above? LFCS is the result of our search for a unique model that is sufficiently general for serving as support for all the various notions and algorithms that will be presented in this work.

Despite its simplicity, LFCS can be used to model easily many different types of systems and communication mechanisms. Several processes can synchronize on the same transition by being active for this transition. This enables one to model two-way rendez-vous (pairwise CCS-like synchronizations) as well as multi-way rendez-vous (multi-process CSP-like synchronizations). Processes can also communicate asynchronously by performing operations on shared objects, like shared variables, or semaphores. Message-passing communication is possible via objects modeling FIFO buffers.

LFCS can be viewed as an extension of the *formal concurrent systems* (FCS) of [Gri90], itself being inspired by a formalism used in [Sif82]. In FCS, transitions are not labeled, no particular initial state is associated with a system, and objects (called variables in FCS) are just memory locations without a general notion of operation. FCS is presented in [Gri93] as a trade-off between CSP [Hoa85] and UNITY [CM88], which are both related to Dijkstra's Guarded Command language [Dij76]. Indeed, FCS (and LFCS) is structured into processes as in CSP, while the notion of parallel composition of processes is avoided as in UNITY by explicitly representing synchronizations between processes by "joint" transitions, i.e., transitions for which several processes are active. In this way, (L)FCS can represent concurrent systems independently of a particular semantics of parallel composition of processes. LFCS has also similarities with Petri Nets [Pet81, Rei85]. By removing the set $\mathcal{O}$ of objects in a LFCS, one obtains a contact-free one-safe Petri Net in which the number of tokens remains permanently equal to the number n of processes, and whose transitions are labeled with symbols in Σ.

One could wonder why objects have been introduced in LFCS. Indeed, since the set of possible values for all objects is assumed to be finite, objects could be represented by finite-state processes. However, in practice, representing objects by processes is tedious. For example, a variable whose value can range on a finite domain V would be represented by a process containing as many local states as there are possible different values for the variable, i.e., $|V|$ states. Objects enable one to model data structures more compactly and directly.

Another, more fundamental, reason for using objects is that control should be clearly distinguished from data in the modeling of concurrent reactive systems. Indeed, the properties one wants to check on such systems are often properties that involve only the control part of the processes of the system. Hence, control is of primary interest during the analysis of such systems, while data are relevant only if they influence the control part of the processes. Therefore, distinguishing control from data in the model itself can help to identify what is relevant for the verification of a given property, and what is not. We will show that the methods developed in this work are able to take advantage of these information to make verification more efficient.

For a similar reason, the notion of process is important in LFCS: information about which process is active for which transition is exploited by some of the algorithms that will be presented later to further improve the verification (see Chapter 4). The reason why transitions in a LFCS are labeled will also appear later, in Chapter 7.

Chapter 3

Using Partial Orders to Tackle State Explosion

When the global state space A_G of a system is finite, it is theoretically possible to explore the whole of A_G in order to check properties of the system. In practice, this is often not the case: A_G is frequently much too large to be exhaustively explored. This phenomenon is called the *state-explosion problem*.

One cause of the state-explosion problem is the modeling of concurrency by interleaving: all interleavings of all concurrent transitions of the system are represented in A_G. In this chapter, we show that exploring all these interleavings is not necessary for verification.

3.1 Independent Transitions

The intuition behind the methods developed in this work is that concurrent executions are really partial orders where concurrent "independent" transitions should be left unordered. When can transitions be considered as independent? The intuitive idea is that transitions are independent when the order of their occurrence is irrelevant.

This notion of independency between transitions and its complementary notion, the notion of dependency, can be formalized by the following definition (adapted from [KP92a]).

Definition 3.1 Let T be the set of transitions in a LFCS and $D \subseteq T \times T$ be a binary, reflexive, and symmetric relation. The relation D is a *valid dependency relation* for the LFCS iff for all $t_1, t_2 \in T$, $(t_1, t_2) \notin D$ (t_1 and t_2 are independent) implies that the two following properties hold for all global states $s \in S$ of the LFCS:

1. if t_1 is enabled in s and $s \xrightarrow{t_1} s'$, then t_2 is enabled in s iff t_2 is enabled in s' (independent transitions can neither disable nor enable each other); and

2. if t_1 and t_2 are enabled in s, then there is a unique state s' such that $s \xrightarrow{t_1 t_2} s'$ and $s \xrightarrow{t_2 t_1} s'$ (commutativity of enabled independent transitions).

∎

This definition characterizes the properties of possible "valid" dependency relations for the transitions of a given LFCS. One can wonder if this definition is of more than semantic use. Indeed, it is not practical to check the two properties listed above for all pairs of transitions for all states in order to determine which transitions are independent and which are not. Fortunately, in practice, it is possible to give easily checkable *syntactic* conditions that are *sufficient* for transitions to be *independent*.

For instance, with LFCS, a sufficient syntactic condition for two transitions t_1 and t_2 in T to be independent is that:

1. the set of processes that are active for t_1 is disjoint from the set of processes that are active for t_2, *and*

2. the set of objects that are accessed by t_1 is disjoint from the set of objects that are accessed by t_2.

It is easy to see that the dependency relation induced by the above syntactic condition is a valid one. Detecting independency in concurrent systems is further discussed in Section 3.4.

Note 3.2 With the LFCS model we have chosen for representing concurrent systems, each global transition in the global state space of a system corresponds to the execution of exactly one transition appearing in the representation of the system, i.e., one element of the set T of the LFCS. With models that include a notion of parallel composition of processes, the correspondence between global transitions and transitions that appear in the description of a system is less straightforward. Indeed, this correspondence depends on the semantics of the parallel composition, which determine how several transitions of different processes can be synchronized to form one global transition. Such global transitions can then be grouped into "system transitions", on which dependency relations can be defined [GW93]. ∎

3.2 Traces

Following the work of Mazurkiewicz [Maz86], one can use the notion of independent transitions to define an equivalence relation on sequences of transitions: *two sequences of transitions are equivalent if they can be obtained from each other by successively permuting adjacent independent transitions.* Thus, given a valid dependency relation, sequences of transitions can be grouped into equivalence classes which Mazurkiewicz calls *traces*.

Formally, Mazurkiewicz's traces are defined as follows [Maz86].

Definition 3.3 A *concurrent alphabet* is a pair $\Lambda = (\mathcal{T}, D)$ where $\mathcal{T}$ is a finite set of symbols (here transitions), called the alphabet of Λ, and where D is a binary, reflexive, and symmetric relation on $\mathcal{T}$ called the *dependency* in Λ. ∎

The relation $I_\Lambda = \mathcal{T}^2 \setminus D$ stands for the *independency* in Λ.

Definition 3.4 Let $\Lambda = (\mathcal{T}, D)$ be a concurrent alphabet, let $\mathcal{T}^*$ represent the set of all finite sequences (words) of symbols in $\mathcal{T}$, let $\cdot$ stand for the concatenation operation, and let ε denote the empty word. We define the relation $\equiv_\Lambda$ as the least congruence in the monoid $[\mathcal{T}^*; \cdot, \varepsilon]$ such that

$$(t_1, t_2) \in I_\Lambda \Rightarrow t_1 t_2 \equiv_\Lambda t_2 t_1.$$

∎

The relation $\equiv_\Lambda$ is referred to as the *trace equivalence over* Λ. $[\mathcal{T}^*; \cdot, \varepsilon]$ is a monoid in which the concatenation operation $\cdot$ may be commutative for some pairs of different elements. It is sometimes called a free partially commutative monoid over $\mathcal{T}$.

Definition 3.5 Equivalence classes of $\equiv_\Lambda$ are called *traces over* Λ. ∎

The trace containing a sequence of transitions w will be denoted $[w]_{(\mathcal{T},D)}$ or $[w]$ for short when there is no ambiguity. A trace is fully characterized by one of its sequences w and a concurrent alphabet $\Lambda = (\mathcal{T}, D)$: by successively permuting adjacent independent transitions in w, one can obtain all the other sequences in $[w]$.

In Mazurkiewicz's trace semantics, the behavior of a concurrent system is defined as a set of traces. Mazurkiewicz's trace semantics is often referred to as being a *partial-order semantics* because it is possible to define a correspondence between traces and partial orders of occurrences of transitions [Maz86].

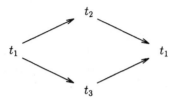

Figure 3.1: Partial order of transition occurrences

Definition 3.6 A relation $R \subseteq A \times A$ on a set A that is reflexive, antisymmetric, and transitive is called a *partial order*. A partial order $R \subseteq A \times A$ is also a *total order* if, for all $a_1, a_2 \in A$, either $(a_1, a_2) \in R$ or $(a_2, a_1) \in R$ [LP81]. ■

A partial order $R \subseteq A \times A$ can be represented graphically by a directed graph whose vertices are elements of A and whose edges are elements of R: $(a_1, a_2) \in R$ iff there is an edge from a_1 to a_2.

Definition 3.7 A *linearization* of a partial order $R \subseteq A \times A$ is a total order $R' \subseteq A \times A$ such that $R' \supseteq R$. ■

The following theorem states that a partial order can be represented by the set of its linearizations (e.g., [Pra86]).

Theorem 3.8 *The intersection of all the linearizations of a partial order is that partial order.*

A correspondence between traces and partial orders of transition occurrences can be defined in such a way that *the set of transition sequences in the trace is the set of all linearizations of the partial order of transition occurrences.*

Example 3.9 Consider the set $T = \{t_1, t_2, t_3\}$ of transitions, and assume that t_1 is dependent with respect to t_2 and t_3, while t_2 and t_3 are independent: we have $D = \{(t_1, t_1), (t_2, t_2), (t_3, t_3), (t_1, t_2), (t_2, t_1), (t_1, t_3), (t_3, t_1)\}$. Then, the sequence $w = t_1 t_2 t_3 t_1$ of transitions defines the trace $[w] = \{t_1 t_2 t_3 t_1, t_1 t_3 t_2 t_1\}$ (the second sequence $t_1 t_3 t_2 t_1$ can be obtained from the first sequence $t_1 t_2 t_3 t_1$ by permuting the two adjacent independent transitions t_2 and t_3 in the first sequence). The sequence w contains 4 transition occurrences. Consider the partial order $R \subseteq A \times A$ that is graphically represented in Figure 3.1: vertices are elements of A (transition occurrences), while edges are elements of R (edges implied by transitivity or reflexivity are omitted in Figure 3.1). The set of all linearizations of this partial order of transition occurrences coincides with the set of transition sequences in $[w]$. ∎

By definition, all transition sequences in a given trace contain the same number of transitions. Moreover, we have the following.

Theorem 3.10 *Let s be a state in A_G. If $s \overset{w_1}{\Rightarrow} s_1$ and $s \overset{w_2}{\Rightarrow} s_2$ in A_G, and if $[w_1] = [w_2]$, then $s_1 = s_2$.*

Proof:

By definition, all $w' \in [w]$ can be obtained from w by successively permuting pairs of *adjacent* independent transitions. It is thus sufficient to prove that, for any two words w_1 and w_2 that differ only by the order of *two* adjacent independent transitions, if $s \overset{w_1}{\Rightarrow} s'$ then $s \overset{w_2}{\Rightarrow} s'$.

Let us thus assume that $w = t_1 \ldots ab \ldots t_n$ and $w' = t_1 \ldots ba \ldots t_n$. We have

$$s \overset{t_1}{\to} s_1 \overset{t_2}{\to} s_2 \ldots \overset{t_i}{\to} s_i \overset{a}{\to} s_{i+1} \overset{b}{\to} s_{i+2} \ldots \overset{t_n}{\to} s_n$$

and

$$s \overset{t_1}{\to} s_1 \overset{t_2}{\to} s_2 \ldots \overset{t_i}{\to} s_i \overset{b}{\to} s'_{i+1} \overset{a}{\to} s'_{i+2} \ldots \overset{t_n}{\to} s'_n.$$

Since a and b are independent, it follows that $s_{i+2} = s'_{i+2}$. Since the transitions in w_1 from s_{i+2} and the transitions in w_2 from s'_{i+2} are identical, we have $s_n = s'_n$. ∎

3.3   Selective Search

From Theorem 3.10, it follows that, in order to determine if a state is reachable by any sequence of transitions in a trace, it is sufficient to explore only *one* sequence in that trace. This property is fundamentally what will allow us to explore only a reduced part of the global state space A_G of a system in order to prove properties of that system.

Indeed, consider for instance the problem of detecting deadlocks, i.e., terminating states. A deadlock in a system is a state that is reachable from the initial state s_0 of the system and where all processes are blocked. Formally, one has:

Definition 3.11 A state s in A_G is a *deadlock* iff there is no transition from s in A_G.
∎

If there is a deadlock d in A_G, there is a sequence w of transitions from s_0 to d in A_G, and hence a trace $[w]$ from s_0 to d in A_G. Since all sequences $w' \in [w]$ also lead from s_0 to d, it is sufficient to explore only one of the w' in $[w]$ to visit d, and thus to detect it.

Consequently, it is sufficient to explore *only one* interleaving for each trace the system can execute from its initial state in order to detect all deadlocks d in this system. Deadlock detection is thus reduced to the problem of exploring (at least) one interleaving per "maximal" trace the system can execute from its initial state.

The latter problem can be solved by performing what we call a *selective search* in A_G. A selective search operates as a classical state-space search except that, at each state s reached during the search, it computes a subset T of the set of transitions that are enabled in s, and explores only the transitions in T, the other enabled transitions being not explored. Clearly, a selective search through A_G only reaches a subset (not necessarily proper) of the states and transitions in A_G. If, in each visited state s, the first transition of (at least) one interleaving per trace leading to a deadlock is selected in the set T of transitions to be explored from s, all deadlocks in A_G will eventually be visited by such a selective search.

In the next two chapters, we develop two techniques for computing such sets T: "persistent sets" and "sleep sets". The specification of the algorithms we present in Chapters 4 and 5 is thus that they should find all deadlocks in A_G while exploring as small a fraction as possible of A_G. The verification of more general properties than deadlock detection will be discussed in Chapters 6 and 7.

Before turning to the presentation of persistent sets and sleep sets, let us further discuss how to detect independency in the description of concurrent systems.

Note 3.12 It might appear that we are using Mazurkiewicz's trace semantics, i.e., that we consider that the behavior of a system is the set of all possible traces it can execute from its initial state. This is not really so. Indeed, to view Mazurkiewicz's theory as a semantics, the dependency relation should be considered as part of the semantics: given a dependency relation, one can determine the Mazurkiewicz seman-tics of a system. The criterion for a partial construction of the state space would then be that the Mazurkiewicz's trace semantics are preserved. Here a less restrictive point of view is taken. Indeed, our only requirement on selective searches is that they visit enough interleavings to make checking the desired property possible. The link with Mazurkiewicz's trace semantics is only in the fact that the algorithms presented in the next chapters rely on the concept of independency and on the properties it implies, especially Theorem 3.10. ∎

3.4 Detecting Independency in Concurrent Systems

3.4.1 Towards More Independency

The algorithms presented in this work take advantage of the independency between transitions that are simultaneously enabled in order to avoid exploring all their interleavings, and thus to avoid exploring parts of the state space. It is therefore desirable to be able to detect independency between transitions as efficiently as possible.

In Section 3.1, we gave the following sufficient syntactic condition for two transitions t_1 and t_2 in T to be independent in our LFCS model.

> A sufficient syntactic condition for two transitions t_1 and t_2 in T to be independent is that:
>
> 1. the set of processes that are active for t_1 is disjoint from the set of processes that are active for t_2, *and*
>
> 2. the set of objects that are accessed by t_1 is disjoint from the set of objects that are accessed by t_2.

Intuitively, "dependency" may arise between two transitions because of either their control part (point 1) or their data part (point 2).

We now discuss how more discriminating criteria can be developed.

For instance, point 1 of the above condition could be replaced by the new condition:

$$(pre(t_1) \cup post(t_1)) \cap (pre(t_2) \cup post(t_2)) = \emptyset.$$

Indeed, it is easy to show that this new condition also induces a valid dependency relation, i.e., that two transitions t_1 and t_2 that satisfy the new condition and that do not both access a common object cannot enable nor disable each other, and are commutative. Moreover, this new condition is weaker than the previous one. Indeed, two transitions t_1 and t_2 that satisfy point 1 above also satisfy the new condition, while the converse is not true (e.g., consider the two transitions $t_1 = (\{l_1\}, G_1, C_1, \{l_2\})$ and $t_2 = (\{l_3\}, G_2, C_2, \{l_4\})$ such that l_1, l_2, l_3, l_4 are local states of a same process). Hence, one might think that using the new condition is preferable. Maybe surprisingly, this is not the case. Indeed, as will appear in the next chapters, what actually matters is to have as few dependencies as possible between transitions *that may be simultaneously enabled*. Since it can be shown that two transitions t_1 and t_2 that satisfy the new condition but that do not satisfy point 1 above cannot be simultaneously enabled, this particular refinement of point 1 is actually useless (see Section 4.3).

Concerning point 2, "dependency" may arise if t_1 and t_2 access a *common* object. Now, not every pair of operations on an object need be considered as dependent. Thus we can obtain more independency by considering not only which objects a transition accesses, but also which operations on these objects the transition performs.

We thus introduce the following definition of a valid dependency relation between the operations on an object.

Definition 3.13 Let $O = (V, OP)$ be an object, and $D_O \subseteq OP \times OP$ be a binary and symmetric relation. The relation D_O is a *valid dependency relation* for O iff for all $op_1, op_2 \in OP$, $(op_1, op_2) \notin D_O$ (op_1 and op_2 are independent) implies that the two following properties hold for all values $v \in V$, and for all inputs in_1 and in_2:

1. if $op_1(in_1, v)$ is defined, with $op_1(in_1, v) \to (out_1, v_1')$, then $op_2(in_2, v)$ is defined iff $op_2(in_2, v_1')$ is defined; and

2. if $op_1(in_1, v)$ and $op_2(in_2, v)$ are defined, then $\exists out_1, out_2, v_1', v_2', v''$ such that:

   - $op_1(in_1, v) \to (out_1, v_1')$ and $op_2(in_2, v_1') \to (out_2, v'')$; and
   - $op_2(in_2, v) \to (out_2, v_2')$ and $op_1(in_1, v_2') \to (out_1, v'')$

   (commutativity of operations, together with preservation of the outputs).

∎

Example 3.14 Consider again the example of an object representing a boolean value. A valid dependency relation between the operations on this object is given in the following table, where "+" means that operations are dependent, while "–" denotes the fact that operations are independent:

DEP.	$Write$	$Read$
$Write$	$+$	$+$
$Read$	$+$	$-$

Two $Write$ operations are dependent because they can result in the object having different values depending on the order of their execution. A $Read$ and a $Write$ operations are dependent because the output of the $Read$ can be different depending on the order of execution of these operations. Two $Read$ operations are independent because they are always defined and return the same output independently of the order of their execution. ∎

Now, we can define a dependency relation between transitions in a LFCS from dependency relations between operations.

Definition 3.15 Let $\mathcal{T}$ be the set of transitions in a LFCS. Two transitions $t_1, t_2 \in \mathcal{T}$ are *independent* if:

1. the set of processes that are active for t_1 is disjoint from the set of processes that are active for t_2, and

2. $\forall op_1 \in used(t_1)$ and $\forall op_2 \in used(t_2)$, if op_1 and op_2 are two operations on a same object, then op_1 and op_2 are independent.

∎

One can easily check that the dependency relation on transitions obtained with this definition is weaker than the one of Section 3.1 and is a valid one. But, it is possible to go further.

3.4.2 Refining Dependencies between Operations

In practice, there are essentially two ways of refining dependencies between operations: by *refining the operations* themselves and by *using conditional dependency* [GP93].

Refining an operation op_i consists of splitting the operation viewed as a set of pairs $(IN_i \times V, OUT_i \times V)$ in several parts, and considering these different parts as being different operations, between which some independency may arise.

Example 3.16 Consider again the example of the object corresponding to a boolean variable. We saw that, in general, two $Write$ operations are dependent. But there are special cases of $Write$ operations that can be considered as being independent: for instance, two complementation operations $Compl$, formally defined by $Compl(-,0) \rightarrow (-,1)$ and $Compl(-,1) \rightarrow (-,0)$ (always defined), can be considered as being independent according to Definition 3.13. We obtain a new dependency relation:

DEP.	$Write$	$Compl$	$Read$
$Write$	+	+	+
$Compl$	+	−	+
$Read$	+	+	−

∎

In the previous example, the new dependency relation obtained after refining the operation $Write$ may yield less dependencies between the transitions of the program. It is thus preferable to use $Compl$ rather than $Write$ whenever possible. In practice, this can be done by adding the operation $Compl$ to the modeling language and by using it explicitly in the description of the system, or the verification tool could detect automatically when a $Write$ operation actually performs a $Compl$ operation.

The second way of refining dependency relations is to define them as being *conditional*: instead of defining a dependency relation that holds for all states s in A_G, it is possible to define a dependency relation for each state individually [KP92a]. Definition 3.1 then becomes:

Definition 3.17 Let $\mathcal{T}$ be the set of transitions in a LFCS and $D \subseteq \mathcal{T} \times \mathcal{T} \times S$. The relation D is a *valid conditional dependency relation* for the LFCS iff for all $t_1, t_2 \in \mathcal{T}, s \in S$, $(t_1, t_2, s) \notin D$ (t_1 and t_2 are independent in s) implies that $(t_2, t_1, s) \notin D$ and that the two following properties hold in state s:

1. if t_1 is enabled in s and $s \xrightarrow{t_1} s'$, then t_2 is enabled in s iff t_2 is enabled in s' (independent transitions can neither disable nor enable each other); and

2. if t_1 and t_2 are enabled in s, then there is a unique state s' such that $s \xrightarrow{t_1 t_2} s'$ and $s \xrightarrow{t_2 t_1} s'$ (commutativity of enabled independent transitions).

∎

Definition 3.13 can be adapted in a similar way as follows.

Definition 3.18 Let $O = (V, OP)$ be an object, and $D_O \subseteq OP \times OP \times V$. The relation D_O is a *valid conditional dependency relation* for O iff for all $op_1, op_2 \in OP, v \in V$, $(op_1, op_2, v) \notin D_O$ (op_1 and op_2 are independent for v) implies that $(op_2, op_1, v) \notin D_O$ and that the two following properties hold for v, and for all inputs in_1 and in_2:

1. if $op_1(in_1, v)$ is defined, with $op_1(in_1, v) \rightarrow (out_1, v_1')$, then $op_2(in_2, v)$ is defined iff $op_2(in_2, v_1')$ is defined; and

2. if $op_1(in_1, v)$ and $op_2(in_2, v)$ are defined, then $\exists out_1, out_2, v_1', v_2', v''$ such that:

   - $op_1(in_1, v) \rightarrow (out_1, v_1')$ and $op_2(in_2, v_1') \rightarrow (out_2, v'')$; and
   - $op_2(in_2, v) \rightarrow (out_2, v_2')$ and $op_1(in_1, v_2') \rightarrow (out_1, v'')$

   (commutativity of operations, with the same outputs).

∎

Note that, in Definition 3.18, dependency is defined for two operations on the same object for a particular value v of the object, but for all inputs the operations can have. This could be also refined in a similar way by considering different possible inputs separately, etc. For the sake of simplicity, this refinement will not be considered here.

In what follows, two operations on an object O_j, $1 \leq j \leq m$, will be said to be independent in state s iff they are independent for the value $v \in V_j$ of the object O_j in state s.

Example 3.19 Consider an object representing a bounded FIFO channel (buffer) of size N. The domain V of possible values for this object is the set of sequences of messages $\{\emptyset\} \cup M \cup M^2 \cup \ldots \cup M^N$, where M is the set of messages that can be transmitted via the channel. We define three operations *Send*, *Receive* and *Length* on this object such that:

- $Send(v, v_1 v_2 \ldots v_n) \rightarrow (-, v_1 v_2 \ldots v_n v)$ defined if $n < N$ and $v \in M$,

- $Receive(-, v_1 v_2 \ldots v_n) \rightarrow (v_1, v_2 \ldots v_n)$ defined if $n > 0$,

- $Length(-, v_1 v_2 \ldots v_n) \rightarrow (n, v_1 v_2 \ldots v_n)$ always defined.

The following tables give respectively a constant and a conditional dependency relation between these operations. If the condition given in the row *op* and column *op'* of the table is true for the value $v \in V$ considered (n is the number of messages in the channel), then op and op' are dependent for v. Otherwise, they are independent. A "–" in the table represents a condition which is always false (operations always independent).

DEP.	Send	Receive	Length
Send	+	+	+
Receive	+	+	+
Length	+	+	–

DEP.	Send	Receive	Length
Send	$n < N$	$n = 0$ or $n = N$	$n < N$
Receive	$n = 0$ or $n = N$	$n > 0$	$n > 0$
Length	$n < N$	$n > 0$	–

Thanks to conditional dependency, operations that are dependent for some but not all values $v \in V$ are no more considered as being dependent for all values. ∎

We can still reduce dependencies between operations by simultaneously refining the operations and by using conditional dependency.

Example 3.20 Consider the previous example. In real protocol models, the operation *Length* is often used to test if a channel is empty or full [GP93]. Let us introduce two new operations *Empty* and *Full* defined as follows:

- $Empty(-, v_1 v_2 \ldots v_n) \rightarrow$ (if ($n = 0$) then *true* else *false*, $v_1 v_2 \ldots v_n$) always defined.

- $Full(-, v_1 v_2 \ldots v_n) \rightarrow$ (if ($n = N$) then *true* else *false*, $v_1 v_2 \ldots v_n$) always defined.

A new dependency relation can then be defined:

DEP.	Send	Receive	Length	Empty	Full
Send	$n < N$	$n = 0$ or $n = N$	$n < N$	$n = 0$	$n = N - 1$
Receive	$n = 0$ or $n = N$	$n > 0$	$n > 0$	$n = 1$	$n = N$
Length	$n < N$	$n > 0$	–	–	–
Empty	$n = 0$	$n = 1$	–	–	–
Full	$n = N - 1$	$n = N$	–	–	–

∎

Note that, when using a conditional dependency relation, the definition of a trace has to be slightly modified: two sequences

$$s \xrightarrow{t_1} s_1 \ldots \xrightarrow{t_i} s_i \xrightarrow{a} s_{i+1} \xrightarrow{b} s_{i+2} \ldots \xrightarrow{t_n} s_n$$

and

$$s \xrightarrow{t_1} s_1 \ldots \xrightarrow{t_i} s_i \xrightarrow{b} s'_{i+1} \xrightarrow{a} s'_{i+2} \ldots \xrightarrow{t_n} s'_n$$

in A_G belong to the same "conditional trace $[t_1 \ldots t_n]$ from state s in A_G", denoted $[t_1 \ldots t_n]_s$, if a and b are independent *in state s_i*. Conditional traces are thus equivalence classes of transition sequences originating *from the same state in A_G*.

It is pointed out in [KP92a] that, maybe surprisingly, a conditional trace does not necessarily correspond anymore to a partial order of transition occurrences: the set of sequences in a conditional trace does not always correspond to the set of all linearizations of a partial order. However, Theorem 3.10 is still satisfied by conditional traces (just replace in the proof "a and b are independent" by "a and b are independent in s_i"). Since the preservation of this theorem is the main assumption about traces which is needed by the algorithms we develop in the sequel of this work, we will not distinguish traces from conditional traces unless otherwise specified.

3.4.3 Summary

A valid conditional dependency relation between the transitions of a LFCS can be defined from valid conditional dependency relations between operations on objects as follows.

Definition 3.21 Let $\mathcal{T}$ be the set of transitions in a LFCS. Two transitions $t_1, t_2 \in \mathcal{T}$ are *independent* in state $s \in S$ if:

1. the set of processes that are active for t_1 is disjoint from the set of processes that are active for t_2, and

2. $\forall op_1 \in used(t_1)$ and $\forall op_2 \in used(t_2)$, if op_1 and op_2 are two operations on the same object, then op_1 and op_2 are independent in s.

■

Since we assumed in Section 2.1 that, in the command of a transition, an operation that modifies the value of a given object cannot be followed by any other operation on this object in the remainder of the sequence of operations defining the command, it is easy to show that the conditional dependency relation on transitions obtained with the above definition is a valid one.

In practice, valid dependency relations between all possible operations on each type of shared (communication) objects are defined as carefully as possible once and for all. They can be represented, for instance, by tables like the ones presented in the previous Section. From these tables and Definition 3.21, dependencies between transitions can then be computed directly.

For the sake of generality, we will only consider in the sequel the (more general) case where a valid *conditional* dependency relation between transitions is used, though all the algorithms that are presented in the following chapters can also be used with a valid constant dependency relation between transitions.

In summary, we thus assume in the sequel that, for each type of (communication) objects, a valid conditional dependency relation between all possible operations on the object is given. Then, for each LFCS, a valid conditional dependency relation for the LFCS is obtained by using Definition 3.21 and the valid conditional dependency relations on operations on objects used by the transitions of the LFCS. This valid conditional dependency relation determines the dependencies between all the transitions of the LFCS.

Chapter 4

Persistent Sets

The first technique for computing the set of transitions T to consider in a selective search actually corresponds to a whole family of algorithms [Ove81, Val91, GW91b] that have been proposed independently by several researchers. In this chapter, we show that all these algorithms actually compute *persistent sets*, and compare them with each other. Then we present an algorithm that generalizes the previous ones in a sense that will be given later.

4.1 Definition

Persistent sets were introduced in [GP93]. Intuitively, a subset T of the set of transitions enabled in a state s of A_G is called *persistent in* s if all transitions not in T that are enabled in s, or in a state reachable from s through transitions not in T, are independent with all transitions in T. In other words, whatever one does from s, while remaining outside of T, does not interact with or affect T. Formally, we have the following.

Definition 4.1 A set T of transitions enabled in a state s is *persistent in* s iff, for all nonempty sequences of transitions

$$s = s_1 \xrightarrow{t_1} s_2 \xrightarrow{t_2} s_3 \ldots \xrightarrow{t_{n-1}} s_n \xrightarrow{t_n} s_{n+1}$$

from s in A_G and including only transitions $t_i \notin T$, $1 \leq i \leq n$, t_n is independent in s_n with all transitions in T. ∎

```
1     Initialize:Stack is empty; H is empty;
2              push (s₀) onto Stack;
3     Loop: while Stack ≠ ∅ do {
4              pop (s) from Stack;
5              if s is NOT already in H then {
6                enter s in H;
7                T = Persistent_Set(s);
8                for all t in T do {
9                    s' = succ(s) after t; /* t is executed */
10                   push (s') onto Stack;
11                }
12             }
13    }
```

Figure 4.1: Persistent-set selective search

Note that the set of all enabled transitions in a state s is trivially persistent since nothing is reachable from s by transitions that are not in this set.

Let a *persistent-set selective search* be a selective search through A_G which, in each state s that it reaches, explores only a set T of enabled transitions that is persistent in s, and that is nonempty if there exist transitions enabled in s. Such an algorithm is illustrated in Figure 4.1. Let A_R be the reduced state-space explored by a persistent-set selective search. We now prove that such a search reaches all deadlocks of A_G (cf. Definition 3.11), i.e., all deadlocks in A_G are also present in A_R.

Lemma 4.2 *Let s be a state in A_R, and let d be a deadlock reachable from s in A_G by a nonempty sequence w of transitions. For all $w_i \in [w]_s$, let t_i denote the first transition of w_i. Let Persistent_Set(s) be a nonempty persistent set in s. Then, at least one of the transitions t_i is in Persistent_Set(s).*

Proof:

Let the sequence w of transitions be $t_1 t_2 \ldots t_n$, and let $s = s_1 \xrightarrow{t_1} s_2 \xrightarrow{t_2} s_3 \ldots \xrightarrow{t_{n-1}} s_n \xrightarrow{t_n} d$ be the sequence of states it goes through in A_G. Assume first that none of the transitions in w are in Persistent_Set(s). Then, by Definition 4.1 of persistent sets, for all transitions t_j, $1 \le j \le n$, t_j is independent in s_j with all transitions in

Persistent_Set(s). Thus, by Definition 3.17 of independent transitions, all transitions in Persistent_Set(s) remain enabled in all states s_j, $1 \leq j \leq n$, and in d, which hence cannot be a deadlock. Thus, some transition of the sequence w from s to d must be in Persistent_Set(s).

Let thus t_k be the first transition in w that is in Persistent_Set(s) and let w' be the sequence $t_k t_1 \ldots t_{k-1} t_{k+1} \ldots t_n$, i.e., the sequence w where the transition t_k is moved to the first position. By Definition 4.1 of persistent sets, we have that for all $1 \leq j < k$, t_j is independent with t_k in s_j. Consequently, by definition of a trace, $w' \in [w]_s$, and the lemma is proved. ∎

Theorem 4.3 *Let s be a state in A_R, and let d be a deadlock reachable from s in A_G by a sequence w of transitions. Then, d is also reachable from s in A_R.*

Proof:

The proof proceeds by induction on the length of w. For $|w| = 0$, the result is immediate. Now, assume the theorem holds for paths (sequences of transitions) of length $n \geq 0$ and let us prove that it holds for paths w of length $n + 1$.

Assume a deadlock d can be reached from a state s by a path w of length $n + 1$ in A_G. For all $w_i \in [w]_s$, let t_i denote the first transition of w_i. Let Persistent_Set(s) be the nonempty persistent set that is selected in s by the algorithm of Figure 4.1, i.e., the set of transitions that are explored from s in A_R. From Lemma 4.2, we know that at least one of the transitions t_i is in Persistent_Set(s). Since t_i is in Persistent_Set(s), it is explored from state s and a state from which a path of length n leads to the deadlock d is reached in A_R. This together with the inductive hypothesis proves the theorem. ∎

From Theorem 4.3 it is then immediate to conclude that a persistent-set selective search started in the initial state of A_G will explore all deadlocks in A_G.

4.2 Computing Persistent Sets

Of course, the key element required for the implementation of a persistent-set selective search is an algorithm for computing persistent sets. Several such algorithms have been proposed independently by various researchers [Ove81, Val91, GW91b]. In this chapter, we present these algorithms, and show that they all compute persistent sets.

---

1. **Take one transition** t **that is enabled in** s. **Let** $T = \{t\}$.

2. **For all transitions** t **in** T, **add to** T **all transitions** t' **such that**

   (a) t **and** t' **are in conflict; or**

   (b) t **and** t' **are parallel and** $\exists op \in used(t), \exists op' \in used(t') : op$ **and** op' **can-be-dependent.**

3. **Repeat step 2 until a disabled transition is introduced in** T, **or until no more transitions need be added. If there is a disabled transition in** T, **return the set of all enabled transitions (this algorithm was not able to compute a nontrivial persistent set). Else, return the set** T.

Figure 4.2: Algorithm 1

All these algorithms infer the persistent sets from the static structure (code) of the system being verified. They differ by the type of information about the system description that they use. The aim of these algorithms is to obtain the smallest possible nonempty persistent sets. Usually, the more information about the system description the algorithm uses, the smaller the persistent set it produces can be, albeit at the cost of a higher computational complexity. Note that exploring the smallest number of enabled transitions at each step of the search is only a heuristics: it does not necessary lead to the exploration of the smallest number of states. We will come back to this point in Section 4.8.

4.3   Algorithm 1 (Conflicting Transitions)

The simplest algorithm for computing persistent sets in a state s is certainly the one that merely computes the set of all transitions that are enabled in s. Indeed, as pointed out in the Section 4.1, this set is trivially persistent in s. Of course, the state space A_R explored by a selective search using such an algorithm is then exactly the global state space A_G, which is precisely what we want to avoid.

A simple algorithm for computing *nontrivial* persistent sets, adapted from [GW91b, GW93], is given in Figure 4.2. This algorithm uses the following definitions.

Definition 4.4 Two transitions t_1 and t_2 are said to be *in conflict* iff $(pre(t_1) \cap$

$pre(t_2)) \neq \emptyset$ (there exists a process P_i that is active for both t_1 and t_2, and such that P_i can choose between t_1 and t_2 from its local state $(pre(t_1) \cap pre(t_2) \cap P_i)$). ∎

Definition 4.5 Two transitions t_1 and t_2 are said to be *parallel* iff $(active(t_1) \cap active(t_2)) = \emptyset$ (the set of processes that are active for t_1 is disjoint from the set of processes that are active for t_2). ∎

In practice, checking whether two transitions are in conflict or parallel is a direct syntactic check.

Definition 4.6 Two operations op_1 and op_2 on a same object *can-be-dependent* if there exists a state s in S such that op_1 and op_2 are dependent in s. ∎

(Remember that S is the set of states of the LFCS and that S includes all states in A_G.) In practice, a relation "can-be-dependent" between operations on a given object is easily obtained from the dependency relation between these operations.

The algorithm of Figure 4.2, let us call it Algorithm 1, starts by taking arbitrarily a transition t that is enabled in the current state s (step 1). To build a persistent set T containing t, all transitions that could "interfere" with t have to be included in T. For this reason, transitions that are in conflict with t, and transitions that are parallel and that use operations that can-be-dependent with operations used by t are introduced into T (step 2). Step 2 is repeated until a disabled transition is introduced into T, or until no more transitions need be added (step 3). Then, if all transitions in T are enabled in s, T is returned. Else, Algorithm 1 was not able to compute a persistent set smaller than the set of all enabled transitions in s.

We now prove that Algorithm 1 computes persistent sets.

Theorem 4.7 *Any set of transitions that is returned by Algorithm 1 is a persistent set in the current state s.*

Proof:

Let T' be a set of transitions that is returned by Algorithm 1, and let T denote the set of transitions that have been considered in step 2 of the algorithm during this run. If T contains a disabled transition, T' is the set of all enabled transitions in s, and is trivially persistent in s. Else, $T' = T$, and T contains exclusively enabled transitions.

Suppose that T is not persistent in s. Thus, by Definition 4.1, there exists in A_G a sequence $s = s_1 \xrightarrow{t_1} s_2 \xrightarrow{t_2} s_3 \ldots \xrightarrow{t_{n-1}} s_n \xrightarrow{t_n} s_{n+1}$ of transitions $t_1, t_2, \ldots, t_n \notin T$, such that t_n is dependent in s_n with some transition $t \in T$. Consider the shortest such a sequence. For this sequence, not only t_n is dependent in s_n with some transition $t \in T$, but also, for all $1 \leq i < n$, t_i is independent in s_i with all transitions in T. Let us show that such a sequence cannot exist.

Assume that t and t_n are parallel. We know from Definition 3.21 that a sufficient syntactic condition for two transitions t and t_n to be independent in a state s_n is that they are parallel and $\forall op_1 \in used(t)$ and $\forall op_2 \in used(t_n)$, if op_1 and op_2 are two operations on a same object, then op_1 and op_2 are independent in s_n. Since t and t_n are dependent in s_n, this implies that $\exists op \in used(t), \exists op' \in used(t_n) : op$ and op' are dependent in s_n. Consequently, op and op' can-be-dependent according to Definition 4.6. Hence, by step 2.b of the algorithm, t_n has to be included in T, which contradicts the assumption that $t_n \notin T$. Therefore, we conclude that t and t_n are not parallel.

Since t and t_n are not parallel, by Definition 4.5, there exists at least one process P_i that is active for both transitions t and t_n: $P_i \in (active(t) \cap active(t_n))$. Let $s(i)$ denote the local state of process P_i in s (i.e., the ith component of s), and let $s_n(i)$ be the local state of P_i in s_n. Since t is enabled in s and $P_i \in active(t)$, $s(i) \in pre(t)$. Moreover, since t_n is enabled in s_n and $P_i \in active(t_n)$, $s_n(i) \in pre(t_n)$. If t and t_n are in conflict, t_n has to be included in set T by step 2.a of the algorithm, which yield a contradiction with the assumption that T contains exclusively enabled transitions and $t_n \notin T$. Hence, t and t_n are not in conflict. Since t and t_n are not in conflict, we know that $(pre(t) \cap pre(t_n)) = \emptyset$, and thus $s(i) \neq s_n(i)$. This means that, after the execution of the sequence $t_1 t_2 \ldots t_{n-1}$, process P_i has moved from its local state $s(i)$ to its local state $s_n(i)$. Hence, t is disabled in s_n (P_i is not ready to execute t in s_n). Consequently, there exists a transition t_k, $1 \leq k < n$, such that t is enabled in s_k and disabled in s_{k+1}. In other words, t and t_k are dependent in s_k. This contradicts the assumption that for all $1 \leq i < n$, $t_i \notin T$ and t_i is independent in s_i with all transitions in T. ∎

Example 4.8 Consider a system containing two processes $A = \{a_0, a_1, a_2\}$ and $B = \{b_0, b_1\}$, two objects x and y of type "boolean variable", and three transitions

$$t_1 = (a_0, true, x := 1, a_1), \quad t_3 = (b_0, true, y := 1, b_1),$$
$$t_2 = (a_1, true, y := 0, a_2).$$

Consider the state $s = (a_0, b_0, 0, 0) \in A \times B \times V_x \times V_y$. In state s, both transitions t_1 and t_3 are enabled, and a classical search will therefore execute both of them. However, transition t_1 is not in conflict with any other transition. Moreover, t_1 uses only a $Write$ operation on object x, which cannot be accessed by transitions that are parallel with t_1 (object x is "local" to process A). Therefore, running Algorithm 1 with t_1 as the initial enabled transition taken in step 1 of the algorithm returns $\{t_1\}$. Thus, a persistent-set selective search using Algorithm 1 may only execute transition t_1 from state s. ∎

Step 1 of Algorithm 1 is nondeterministic: a transition t that is enabled in s is arbitrarily chosen to start the persistent set construction. For a given state s, let $Algo_1(t)$ denote the persistent set that is returned by Algorithm 1 when t is the enabled transition chosen in step 1 of the algorithm. Assume that, from any transition t, it takes $O(1)$ time to obtain a transition t' satisfying either condition 2.a or 2.b.[1] Since Algorithm 1 stops (step 3) as soon as a disabled transition is introduced in T, step 2 can be executed at most $|enabled(s)|$ times, where $|enabled(s)|$ denotes the number of transitions that are enabled in s. For the same reason, each time step 2 is executed, at most $|enabled(s)|$ transitions t' can be checked and be added to set T. Hence, the worst-case time complexity of $Algo_1(t)$ is $O(|enabled(s)|^2)$.

Let $PS_1(s)$ denote the set of persistent sets in a state s that can be computed by Algorithm 1: $PS_1(s) = \{Algo_1(t)|t \in enabled(s)\}$. In practice, for a given state s, it may be useful to run Algorithm 1 several times with different initial enabled transitions (step 1) in order to compute several persistent sets in s, and then to choose the smallest persistent set that has been obtained. However, given the symmetry of the relation between t and t' in step 2 of Algorithm 1, it is easy to see that, if $Algo_1(t)$ did not encounter any disabled transitions, we have

$$\forall t' \in Algo_1(t) : Algo_1(t') = Algo_1(t).$$

Hence, once $Algo_1(t)$ has been computed, it is useless to compute $Algo_1(t')$ with $t' \in Algo_1(t)$, i.e., to rerun Algorithm 1 with t' as the starting transition, when the computation of $Algo_1(t)$ did not encounter any disabled transitions. Moreover, we also know that the computation of $Algo_1(t')$ with $t' \notin Algo_1(t)$ will not consider again transitions in $Algo_1(t)$. Therefore, the worst-case time complexity to compute the smallest persistent set in $PS_1(s)$, let us denote it by $min(PS_1(s))$, is also $O(|enabled(s)|^2)$.

---

[1] This can be done by using appropriate data structures constructed to encode the relationships between transitions according to conditions 2.a and 2.b.

---

1. **Take one transition t that is enabled in s. Let $P = active(t)$.**

2. **For all processes P_i in P, for all transitions t such that $s(i) \in pre(t)$, add to P all processes P_j such that**

    (a) $P_j \in active(t)$; **or**

    (b) $P_j \in active(t')$ **for some t' such that t and t' are parallel and**
        $\exists op \in used(t), \exists op' \in used(t') : op$ **and** op' **can-be-dependent.**

3. **Repeat step 2 until no more processes need be added. Then, return all transitions t such that $active(t) \subseteq P$ and t is enabled in s.**

Figure 4.3: Algorithm 2

Note 4.9 Algorithm 1 is equivalent to an algorithm that appeared in [GW91b, GW93]. In [GW91b, GW93], concurrent systems were represented by a set of communicating automata, i.e., a parallel composition of sequential processes (no objects). For the particular model and definition of dependency used in [GW91b, GW93], two transitions that are parallel cannot be dependent, and step 2 of Algorithm 1 reduces to point 2.a only, point 2.b can be deleted. It is pointed out in [GW91b, GW93] that Algorithm 1 can be implemented in such a way that its time complexity is the same as the one of the computation of the set of all the transitions that are enabled in s, by interleaving both computations, instead of computing first the set of enabled transitions as implicitly assumed in the above discussion. Finally note that the procedure given in page 420 of [Pel93] is similar to Algorithm 1. ∎

4.4 Algorithm 2 (Overman's Algorithm)

A more elaborate algorithm for computing nontrivial persistent sets is given in Figure 4.3. Let us call it Algorithm 2. This algorithm is an adaptation of an algorithm that appeared in [Ove81]. The algorithm presented in [Ove81] (page 105) only considered concurrent systems composed of "non-cycling" (no loops) and "non-branching" processes communicating exclusively via shared variables. Thus, the correspondence between Algorithm 2 and the one of [Ove81] might seem rather loose. However, the basic algorithmic idea is the same.

Unlike Algorithm 1, Algorithm 2 can consider disabled transitions, and uses information about processes. More precisely, it uses information about which transitions can be accessed by process P_i from its current local state $s(i)$. Algorithm 2 starts by considering the set P of processes that are active for one given enabled transition (step 1). Then, this set P is recursively augmented with all processes that contain a transition that "might interfere" with the next possible transitions of processes in P. Precisely, for all transitions t "originating from" the current local state $s(i)$ of a process P_i in set P, i.e., for all transitions t such that $s(i) \in pre(t)$, all other processes that are active for t, or that are active for a transition t' that is parallel and that uses operations that can-be-dependent with operations used by t, are added to set P (step 2). Step 2 is repeated until no more processes need be added to P (step 3). Finally, all enabled transitions for which processes in P are active are returned.

We now prove that Algorithm 2 computes persistent sets.

Theorem 4.10 *Any set of transitions that is returned by Algorithm 2 is a persistent set in the current state s.*

Proof:

Let T be a set of transitions that is returned by Algorithm 2, and let P denote the set of processes that have been considered in step 2 of the algorithm during this run.

The proof is by contradiction. Suppose that T is not persistent in s. Thus, by Definition 4.1, there exists in A_G a sequence $s = s_1 \xrightarrow{t_1} s_2 \xrightarrow{t_2} s_3 \ldots \xrightarrow{t_{n-1}} s_n \xrightarrow{t_n} s_{n+1}$ of transitions $t_1, t_2, \ldots, t_n \notin T$, such that t_n is dependent in s_n with some transition $t \in T$. Consider the shortest such a sequence. For this sequence, not only t_n is dependent in s_n with some transition $t \in T$, but also, for all $1 \le i < n$, t_i is independent in s_i with all transitions in T. Let us show that such a sequence cannot exist.

Assume that t and t_n are in parallel. We know from Definition 3.21 that a sufficient syntactic condition for two transitions t and t_n to be independent in a state s_n is that they are parallel and $\forall op_1 \in used(t)$ and $\forall op_2 \in used(t_n)$, if op_1 and op_2 are two operations on a same object, then op_1 and op_2 are independent in s_n. Since t and t_n are dependent in s_n, this implies that $\exists op \in used(t), \exists op' \in used(t_n)$: op and op' are dependent in s_n. Consequently, op and op' can-be-dependent according to Definition 4.6. Hence, by step 2.b of the algorithm, we have $active(t_n) \subseteq P$.

Now, assume that t and t_n are not parallel. By Definition 4.5, there exists at least one process P_i that is active for both transitions t and t_n: $P_i \in (active(t) \cap active(t_n))$. Note that, since $t \in T$, $active(t) \subseteq P$, and thus $P_i \in P$. Let $s(i)$ denote the local state of process P_i in s (i.e., the ith component of s), and let $s_n(i)$ be the local state of

P_i in s_n. Since t_n is enabled in s_n and $P_i \in active(t_n)$, $s_n(i) \in pre(t_n)$. If $s(i) = s_n(i)$, by step 2.a of the algorithm, we have again $active(t_n) \subseteq P$.

Consider the case where $s(i) \neq s_n(i)$. Since t is in T, t is enabled in s, and $s(i) \in pre(t)$. Since $s(i) \neq s_n(i)$, t is disabled in s_n (P_i is not ready to execute t in s_n). Consequently, there exists a transition t_k, $1 \leq k < n$, such that t is enabled in s_k and disabled in s_{k+1}. In other words, t and t_k are dependent in s_k. This contradicts the assumption that for all $1 \leq i < n$, $t_i \notin T$ and t_i is independent in s_i with all transitions in T.

In summary, we have $active(t_n) \subseteq P$. If t_n is enabled in s, t_n is in the set T returned by the algorithm, which contradicts the assumption that $t_n \notin T$. Therefore, t_n is disabled in s.

Since t_n is disabled in s and enabled in s_n, there exists a transition t_k, $1 \leq k < n$, such that t_n is disabled in s_k and enabled in s_{k+1}. In other words, t_n and t_k are dependent in s_k. If, for all transitions t_l, $1 \leq l < n$, $(active(t_l) \cap active(t_n)) = \emptyset$, we have $s(i) \in pre(t_n)$ for all $P_i \in active(t_n)$, and $active(t_k) \subseteq P$ by step 2.b of the algorithm (1). Else, there exists a transition t_l, $1 \leq l < n$, such that $P_i \in active(t_n)$ and $P_i \in active(t_l)$. Let t_l be the first such transition in the sequence $t_1 t_2 \ldots t_{n-1}$. We have $s(i) = s_l(i)$ since t_l is the first transition in the sequence $t_1 t_2 \ldots t_{n-1}$ for which P_i is active. Since t_l is enabled in s_l, $s_l(i) \in pre(t_l)$. Since $active(t_n) \subseteq P$, we have $P_i \in P$, and $active(t_l) \subseteq P$ by step 2.a of the algorithm (2). In summary, in both cases (1) and (2), there exists a transition t_m, $1 \leq m < n$ such that $active(t_m) \subseteq P$. If t_m is enabled in s, it is returned by the algorithm and is thus in T, which contradicts the assumption that $t_m \notin T$. Therefore, t_m is disabled in s.

By repeating the same reasoning, one comes to the conclusion that $active(t_1) \subseteq P$. Since t_1 is enabled in s, this means that $t_1 \in T$, which contradicts the assumption that $t_1, \ldots, t_n \notin T$. ∎

Example 4.11 Consider a system containing two processes $A = \{a_0, a_1, a_2, a_3\}$ and $B = \{b_0, b_1\}$, two objects x and y of type "boolean variable", and four transitions

$$t_1 = (a_0, true, x := 1, a_1), \quad t_4 = (b_0, true, y := 1, b_1),$$
$$t_2 = (a_0, x = 1, x := 0, a_3),$$
$$t_3 = (a_1, true, y := 0, a_2).$$

Consider the state $s = (a_0, b_0, 0, 0) \in A \times B \times V_x \times V_y$. In state s, both transitions t_1 and t_4 are enabled, and a classical search will therefore execute both of them. Since transition t_1 is in conflict with transition t_2 which is disabled in s, $Algo_1(t_1) = \{t_1, t_4\}$.

However, Algorithm 2 starting with t_1 as the initial enabled transition taken in step 1 introduces process A in set P. Then, it checks in step 2 if other processes have to be added to P. Since the only process that is active for the two transitions t_1 and t_2 originating from a_0 is A, and since these two transitions only use object x, which is not used by transitions that are parallel with t_1 or t_2, process B does not need be included in P. Therefore, Algorithm 2 returns $\{t_1\}$, and a persistent-set selective search using Algorithm 2 may only execute transition t_1 from state s. ∎

As in Algorithm 1, step 1 of Algorithm 2 is nondeterministic. For a given state s, let $Algo_2(t)$ denote the persistent set that is returned by Algorithm 2 when t is the enabled transition chosen in step 1 of the algorithm. Step 2 of Algorithm 2 can be executed at most $|\mathcal{P}|$ times, where $|\mathcal{P}|$ is the number of processes in the system. Each time step 2 is executed, at most $|\mathcal{P}|$ processes P_j can be added to set P. If we assume that, from any process P_i, it takes $O(1)$ time to obtain a process P_j satisfying either condition 2.a or 2.b[2], the worst-case time complexity for executing step 2 of Algorithm 2 is $O(|\mathcal{P}|^2)$, and, assuming $|enabled(s)|$ smaller than $|\mathcal{P}|^2$, the worst-case time complexity of $Algo_2(t)$ is also $O(|\mathcal{P}|^2)$.

Let $PS_2(s)$ denote the set of persistent sets in a state s that can be computed by Algorithm 2: $PS_2(s) = \{Algo_2(t)|t \in enabled(s)\}$. It is easy to see that

$$\forall t' \in Algo_2(t) : Algo_2(t') \subseteq Algo_2(t).$$

Therefore, it may be useful to rerun Algorithm 2 with transitions t' taken from a persistent set already obtained by a previous run, to determine if this persistent set contains another smaller persistent set. We will come back to this issue at the end of the next Section.

4.5 Algorithm 3 (Stubborn Sets)

4.5.1 Basic Idea

Yet a more elaborate technique for computing persistent sets is the stubborn set technique of Valmari [Val91]. Unlike Algorithm 2, the stubborn set technique also

---

[2]This can be done by using appropriate data structures to encode the relationships between processes according to conditions 2.a and 2.b. For instance, for all possible local states $s(i)$ of each process P_i, a table that tells which processes have to be included in set P when P_i is in its local state $s(i)$ can be computed from the description of the system before the beginning of the search.

uses information about the internal structure of the processes of the system. Before defining stubborn sets, we need the following definition [Val91].

Definition 4.12 Two transitions t_1 and t_2 *do-not-accord* with each other if there exists a state s in S such that t_1 and t_2 are enabled in s and are dependent in s. ∎

Two transitions do-not-accord with each other if there exists a state where they are both enabled and dependent. We can define a similar relation on operations on objects.

Definition 4.13 Two operations op_1 and op_2 on the same object *do-not-accord* with each other if there exists a state s in S such that op_1 and op_2 are defined in s and are dependent in s. ∎

This definition is slightly weaker than Definition 4.6, i.e., the relation do-not-accord is included in the relation can-be-dependent. Indeed, two operations that do-not-accord can-be-dependent, while the converse does not hold, since two operations that are dependent in a state s need not be both defined in that state. In practice, a relation "do-not-accord" between operations on a given object is easily obtained from the dependency relation between these operations.

We now introduce a new definition that will help us to capture the basic algorithmic idea of stubborn sets without referring to a particular model for representing concurrent systems.

Definition 4.14 Let t be a transition that is disabled in a state s. A *necessary enabling set for t in s*, denoted $NES(t, s)$, is a set of transitions such that, for all states s' such that t is enabled in s', for all sequences w of transitions from s to s' in A_G, w contains at least one transition of $NES(t, s)$. ∎

In other words, a necessary enabling set $NES(t, s)$ for t in s is a set of transitions such that t cannot become enabled (in some successor s' of s in A_G) before at least one transition in $NES(t, s)$ is executed.

Stubborn sets[3] can then be defined as follows (adapted from [Val91]; see also Note 4.17 below).

---

[3] "Strong stubborn sets" according to Valmari's terminology. "Weak stubborn sets" will be considered later.

Definition 4.15 A set T_s of transitions is a *stubborn set* in a state s if T_s contains at least one enabled transition, and if for all transitions $t \in T_s$, the two following conditions hold:

1. if t is disabled in s, then all transitions in one necessary enabling set $NES(t, s)$ for t in s are also in T_s;

2. if t is enabled in s, then all transitions t' that do-not-accord with t are also in T_s.

■

A stubborn set T_s in a state s is thus a set of transitions. Transitions in this set can be either enabled or disabled in s. Let T be the set of all transitions in T_s that are enabled in s. By the definition of T_s, T is nonempty. We now prove that T is a persistent set in s.

Theorem 4.16 *Let T be the set of all transitions in a stubborn set T_s in state s that are enabled in s. Then, T is a persistent set in s.*

Proof:

The proof is by contradiction. Suppose that T is not persistent in s. Thus, by Definition 4.1, there exists in A_G a sequence $s = s_1 \xrightarrow{t_1} s_2 \xrightarrow{t_2} s_3 \ldots \xrightarrow{t_{n-1}} s_n \xrightarrow{t_n} s_{n+1}$ of transitions $t_1, t_2, \ldots, t_n \notin T$, such that t_n is dependent in s_n with some transition $t \in T$. Consider the shortest such a sequence. For this sequence, not only t_n is dependent in s_n with some transition $t \in T$, but also, for all $1 \leq i < n$, t_i is independent in s_i with all transitions in T. Let us show that such a sequence cannot exist.

Since $t \in T$, $t \in T_s$ and t is enabled in s. Since, for all $1 \leq i < n$, t_i is independent in s_i with all transitions in T, including t, t remains enabled in all states s_{i+1}. Since t and t_n are both enabled in s_n and are dependent in s_n, they do-not-accord (cf. Definition 4.12), and t_n is in T_s by point 2 of Definition 4.15.

If t_n is enabled in s, then we have $t_n \in T$, which contradicts the assumption that $t_1, \ldots, t_n \notin T$. Thus, t_n is disabled in s. Since t_n is enabled in s_n, there exists a nonempty necessary enabling set $NES(t_n, s)$ for t_n in s, and (at least) one transition t_j, $1 \leq j < n$, is in $NES(t_n, s)$ (cf. Definition 4.14). By point 1 of Definition 4.15, t_j is in T_s. Again, if t_j is enabled in s, then $t_j \in T$, which contradicts the assumption that $t_1, \ldots, t_n \notin T$. Thus, t_j is disabled in s. By repeating the same reasoning, one comes to the conclusion that t_1 is in T_s. Since t_1 is enabled in s, this means that $t_1 \in T$, which contradicts the assumption that $t_1, \ldots, t_n \notin T$. ∎

Stubborn sets can thus be used to compute persistent sets: by taking all transitions in a stubborn set T_s that are enabled in s, one obtains a persistent set.

Note 4.17 The basic algorithmic idea of stubborn sets is captured by Definition 4.15 introduced in this Section. This definition is general, abstract, in the sense that it is independent of any particular model. In contrast, definitions of stubborn sets that appeared in the literature were tailored for particular models like Variable/Transition Systems, Elementary Nets, Place/Transition Nets, Coloured Petri Nets, etc (e.g., see [Val91]). All these particular definitions can be viewed as "implementations" of the general definition we have given in this Section. Algorithm 3 that will be presented in the next Section is such an "implementation" of Definition 4.15 for systems represented by LFCS's. ∎

4.5.2   Algorithm

From the general definition of stubborn sets given above, it is possible to obtain an algorithm for computing stubborn sets T_s for systems represented by LFCS's. To obtain such an "implementation", we need to give a practical way to compute (and thus approximate) the concepts that appear in Definition 4.15.

The resulting algorithm, Algorithm 3, is presented in Figure 4.4. Algorithm 3 starts by taking a transition t that is enabled in s (step 1). To compute a stubborn set containing t, the two rules 2.a and 2.b are applied repeatedly to all transitions introduced in T_s (step 2) until no more transitions need be added (step 3). Then, all the transitions in the T_s that are enabled in s are returned, the other transitions in T_s are discarded.

To prove that Algorithm 3 returns persistent sets in s, thanks to Theorem 4.16, it is sufficient to show that the sets T_s that it computes are stubborn sets in s according to Definition 4.15. To show this, we have to prove that the rules 2.a and 2.b are safe approximations of respectively point 1 and 2 of Definition 4.15, i.e., that enough transitions are included in set T_s by Algorithm 3 to make it a stubborn set in s .

Theorem 4.18 *All sets T_s that are computed by Algorithm 3 are stubborn sets in s.*

1. Take one transition t that is enabled in s. Let $T_s = \{t\}$.

2. For all transitions t in T_s:

    (a) if t is disabled in s, either:

        i. choose a process $P_j \in active(t)$ such that $s(j) \neq (pre(t) \cap P_j)$; then, add to T_s all transitions t' such that $(pre(t) \cap P_j) \in post(t')$.

        ii. choose a condition c_j in the guard G of t that evaluates to false in s; then, for all operations op used by t to evaluate c_j, add to T_s all transitions t' such that $\exists op' \in used(t') : op$ and op' can-be-dependent.

    (b) if t is enabled in s, add to T_s all transitions t' such that

        i. t and t' are in conflict; or

        ii. t and t' are parallel and $\exists op \in used(t), \exists op' \in used(t') :$ op and op' do-not-accord.

3. Repeat step 2 until no more transitions can be added. Then, return all transitions in T_s that are enabled in s (transitions in T_s that are disabled in s are discarded).

Figure 4.4: Algorithm 3

Proof:

Let T_s be a set of transitions that is computed by Algorithm 3. Let us show that T_s is a stubborn set in s.

Consider a transition $t \in T_s$ that is disabled in s. With our LFCS model, a transition $t = (L, G, C, L')$ is disabled in a state s if either there is a process $P_j \in active(t)$ such that $s(j) \neq (L \cap P_j)$ (process P_j that is active for t is not ready to execute transition t from its current local state $s(j)$), or there is a condition c_j in the conjunction G that evaluates to false in s. In the first case, the set of all transitions t' such that $(pre(t) \cap P_j) \in post(t')$ is a necessary enabling set $NES(t, s)$ for t in s (the execution of such a transition t' is necessary to make t enabled). In the second case, the set of all transitions t' that use an operation op' that can-be-dependent with an operation op used to evaluate c_j is a necessary enabling set $NES(t, s)$ for t in s (only the execution of such an operation op' can change the output returned by op, and hence the truth value of c_j).

Consider a transition $t \in T_s$ that is enabled in s. We have to show that the set of all transitions t' that are added to T_s by step 2.b of Algorithm 3 includes all transitions that do-not-accord with t. Consider a transition t' such that t and t' do-not-accord. Let us show that t' is in T_s.

If t and t' are not parallel, this implies by Definition 4.5 that at least one process is active for both transitions t and t': $P_i \in (active(t) \cap active(t'))$. If t and t' are in conflict, t' is added to T_s by step 2.b.i. If t and t' are not in conflict, we know that $(pre(t) \cap pre(t')) = \emptyset$. Therefore, $(pre(t) \cap P_i) \neq (pre(t') \cap P_i)$, and it is impossible for t and t' to be simultaneously enabled (process P_i cannot be in two different local states $(pre(t) \cap P_i)$ and $(pre(t') \cap P_i)$ at the same time), which contradicts the assumption that t and t' do-not-accord.

Assume now that t and t' are parallel. Since t and t' do-not-accord, there exists a state $s' \in S$ where t and t' are enabled in s' and are dependent in s', by Definition 4.12. Moreover, we know from Definition 3.21 that a sufficient syntactic condition for two transitions t and t' to be independent in a state s' is that they are parallel and $\forall op_1 \in used(t)$ and $\forall op_2 \in used(t')$, if op_1 and op_2 are two operations on a same object, then op_1 and op_2 are independent in s_n. Since t and t' are dependent in s', this implies that $\exists op \in used(t), \exists op' \in used(t')$: op and op' are dependent in s'. Moreover, since t and t' are enabled in s', this implies that both op and op' are defined in s'. Consequently, op and op' do-not-accord according to Definition 4.13. Hence, by step 2.b.ii of the algorithm, t' is included in T_s. ∎

Example 4.19 Consider a system containing two processes $A = \{a_0, a_1, a_2\}$ and $B = \{b_0, b_1\}$, two objects x and y of type "boolean variable", and four transitions

$$t_1 = (a_0, true, x := 1, a_1), \quad t_3 = (b_0, true, y := 1, b_1),$$
$$t_2 = (a_1, true, y := 0, a_2), \quad t_4 = (b_1, true, x := 0, b_0).$$

Consider the state $s = (a_1, b_1, 1, 1) \in A \times B \times V_x \times V_y$. In state s, both transitions t_2 and t_4 are enabled. As an exercice, the reader can compute what the persistent sets that can be returned by Algorithms 1 and 2 are. Actually, $Algo_1(t_2) = Algo_1(t_4) = Algo_2(t_2) = Algo_2(t_4) = \{t_2, t_4\}$. In other words, neither Algorithm 1, nor Algorithm 2 are able to return a nontrivial persistent set for this example. Let us investigate how Algorithm 3, in contrast, is able to determine that $\{t_4\}$ is a persistent set in s. Starting with t_4 as the initial enabled transition taken in step 1, Algorithm 3 has to include transition t_1 in T_s by step 2.b since both t_4 and t_1 use a $Write$ operation on object x, and since two $Write$ operations do-not-accord (they are always defined and dependent; cf. Sections 2.1 and 3.4). Since t_1 is disabled in s, and since the only condition for which it is disabled in s is that process A, which is active for it, is not ready to execute it, step 2.b.i adds to T_s all transitions t' such that $a_0 \in post(t')$. There are no such transitions, and the computation of T_s stops. Hence, $Algo_3(t_4) = \{t_4\}$, and a persistent-set selective search using Algorithm 3 may only execute transition t_4 from state s. ■

As in Algorithms 1 and 2, step 1 of Algorithm 3 is nondeterministic. For a given state s, let $Algo_3(t)$ denote a persistent set that is returned by Algorithm 3 when t is the enabled transition chosen in step 1 of the algorithm. During the computation of $Algo_3(t)$, Step 2 of Algorithm 3 can be executed at most $|T|$ times, where $|T|$ is the number of transitions in the system. Each time step 2 is executed, at most $|T|$ transitions t' can be checked and be added to set T_s. If we assume that, from any transition t, it takes $O(1)$ time to obtain a transition t' satisfying either condition 2.a or 2.b, the worst-case time complexity of $Algo_3(t)$ is $O(|T|^2)$.

Note that point 1 of Definition 4.15, and hence step 2.a of Algorithm 3, are also nondeterministic: one can choose arbitrarily any necessary enabling set $NES(t, s)$ for t in s, and then add to T_s all transitions in this set $NES(t, s)$. Therefore, the choice of a $NES(t, s)$ influences the set of transitions that have to be added to T_s, and thus the size of T_s and the number of enabled transitions it contains. A priori, it is not possible to predict what choice will yield the smallest persistent set. In other words, executing Algorithm 3 several times with the same starting enabled transition taken in step 1 of the algorithm may return different persistent sets, if different choices of $NES(t, s)$ are made for disabled transitions in T_s.

To avoid redundant work during successive executions of Algorithm 3 when searching for a minimal persistent set, a systematic approach, investigated in [Val88a, Val88b], consists in viewing each transition in T as a vertex of a directed graph, and each relation of the form "if t is in T_s, then add t' to T_s" according to step 2.a or 2.b as an edge from vertex t to vertex t'. The problem of finding the smallest persistent set that can be computed by Algorithm 3 is then reduced to a graph-theoretic problem. In [Val88b], it is shown that the problem can be solved in $O(|T|^5)$.[4] If the nondeterminism of step 2.a of Algorithm 3 is resolved in a unique way for each disabled transition, then the time complexity becomes linear in the number of edges in the graph described above, i.e., $O(|T|^2)$ [Val88a].[5]

---

[4] This is done by analyzing another directed graph of $O(|T|^2)$ nodes (and hence $O(|T|^4)$ edges) that is interpreted as an "and/or graph"; see [Val88b].

[5] If for all transitions t, the number of transitions t' that satisfy either point 1 or point 2 of Definition 4.15 is bounded by a constant $C < |T|$, the time complexity of the two algorithms becomes $O(C^2|T|^2)$ and $O(C|T|)$ respectively, as assumed in [Val88a, Val88b].

Interestingly, it can be shown that the same technique can be applied to find the smallest persistent set that can be computed by Algorithm 2 (since the only nondeterministic step in Algorithm 2 is step 1): each process is viewed as a vertex of a directed graph, and each relation "if P_i is in P, then add P_j to P" according to step 2.a or 2.b of Algorithm 2 corresponds to an edge from vertex P_i to vertex P_j. The time complexity for computing the smallest persistent set in the set $PS_2(s)$ of persistent sets that can be computed by Algorithm 2 is thus $O(|\mathcal{P}|^2)$.

4.6   Comparison

In this Section, we compare the persistent sets that can be computed by the three algorithms presented in the previous Sections.

For a given state s, let $Algo_i(t)$ denote the persistent set that is returned by Algorithm i when t is the enabled transition chosen in step 1 of Algorithm i, for $i \in \{1, 2\}$. We can prove the following.

Theorem 4.20 *For all transitions t that are enabled in a state s, we have $Algo_2(t) \subseteq Algo_1(t)$.*

Proof:

If $Algo_1(t)$ is the set of all transitions that are enabled in s, the result is immediate. Thus, assume this is not the case. This means that the set T of transitions constructed in step 2 of Algorithm 1 during the computation of $Algo_1(t)$ contains only enabled transitions, and we have $Algo_1(t) = T$. Let P denote the set of processes that have been considered in step 2 of Algorithm 2 during the computation of $Algo_2(t)$. Let T_s^2 be the set $\{t \mid \exists P_i \in P : s(i) \in pre(t)\}$. By construction, $Algo_2(t)$ is the set of all transitions in T_s^2 that are enabled in s. We now prove that, for all transitions $t \in T$, if $t \in T_s^2$, then all transitions t' that are added to T_s^2 because of t by step 2 of Algorithm 2 are in T.

If t' is added to T_s^2 because of t by step 2.a of Algorithm 2, this means that there exists a process $P_j \in P$ such that $P_j \in active(t)$ and $s(j) \in pre(t')$. Since t is enabled in s, $s(j) \in pre(t)$, and t and t' are in conflict. Consequently, t' is in T by step 2.a of Algorithm 1.

If t' is added to T_s^2 because of t by step 2.b of Algorithm 2, this means that there exists a process $P_j \in P$ such that $s(j) \in pre(t')$ and $P_j \in active(t'')$ for some t'' such that t and t'' are parallel and $\exists op \in used(t), \exists op' \in used(t'')$: op and op' can-be-dependent. Consequently, by step 2.b of Algorithm 1, t'' is in T. Hence, t'' is enabled in s, and we have $s(j) \in pre(t'')$. This implies that t'' is in T_s^2. This also implies that t'' and t' are in conflict, and t' is in T by step 2.a of Algorithm 1.

We have just proved that, for all transitions $t \in T$, if $t \in T_s^2$, then all transitions that are added to T_s^2 because of t by step 2 of Algorithm 2 are in T. Consequently, $T_s^2 \subseteq T$, and thus $Algo_2(t) \subseteq Algo_1(t)$. ∎

Thus, the persistent set $Algo_2(t)$ returned by Algorithm 2 is always a subset (not necessarily proper) of the persistent set $Algo_1(t)$ returned by Algorithm 1.

A similar relation holds between Algorithm 2 and 3, except that, since step 2.a of Algorithm 3 is nondeterministic, the formulation of the theorem has to be slightly modified.

Theorem 4.21 *For all transitions t that are enabled in a state s, there exists an execution of Algorithm 3 that returns a persistent set $Algo_3(t)$ such that $Algo_3(t) \subseteq Algo_2(t)$.*

Proof:

Let P denote the set of processes that have been considered in step 2 of Algorithm 2 during the computation of $Algo_2(t)$. Let T_s^2 be the set $\{t \,|\, \exists P_i \in P : s(i) \in pre(t)\}$. By construction, $Algo_2(t)$ is the set of all transitions in T_s^2 that are enabled in s. If T_s is a stubborn set constructed by Algorithm 3 during the computation of a persistent set $Algo_3(t)$, let T_s^3 denote the transitions t in T_s such that $\exists P_i : s(i) \in pre(t)$. In other words, T_s^3 contains all transitions (enabled or disabled) in T_s that are originating from the current local state of some process (not necessarily in P). Note that all transitions in T_s that are enabled in s are in T_s^3. Moreover, transitions that are in T_s and in T_s^2 are in T_s^3. To prove the theorem, we show that there exists a run of Algorithm 3 such that all enabled transitions in T_s^3 are in T_s^2. This amounts to constructing a set T_s^3 such that, for all transitions $t \in T_s^2$, if $t \in T_s^3$, then all enabled transitions that are added to T_s^3 because of t by (possibly several applications of) step 2 of Algorithm 3 are in T_s^2.

Consider a transition $t \in T_s^3$ that is enabled in s. Since t is in T_s^2, we know $active(t) \subseteq P$. If t' is added to T_s because of t by step 2.b.i of Algorithm 3, this means that t and t' are in conflict. Hence, there exists a process P_i active for t such that $s(i) \in pre(t')$. Since $P_i \in P$, t' is in T_s^2, by definition of T_s^2. Moreover, since t' is in both T_s and T_s^2, it is also in T_s^3.

If t' is added to T_s because of t by step 2.b.ii of Algorithm 3, this means that t and t' are parallel and $\exists op \in used(t), \exists op' \in used(t')$: op and op' do-not-accord. Thus, op and op' can-be-dependent, since the relation do-not-accord is included in the relation can-be-dependent. Consequently, by step 2.b of Algorithm 2, the processes in $active(t')$ are in P. If there is a process P_i such that $s(i) \in pre(t')$, t' is in T_s^2. If for all processes P_i in $active(t')$, $s(i) \notin pre(t')$, t' is disabled in s and is neither in T_s^2, nor in T_s^3. Let P_i be one of the processes active for t'. By applying repeatedly step 2.a.i of Algorithm 3 and choosing P_i, a transition t'' in T_s^2 may eventually be included in set T_s. In this case, intermediate transitions t''' that are included in set T_s during these successive applications of step 2.a.i are all disabled in s, since they are not in T_s^2 (by construction), and hence process P_i, which is active for all these transitions, is not ready to execute any of them: $s(i) \notin pre(t''')$. Since t'' is in both T_s and T_s^2, it is also in T_s^3.

Consider a transition $t \in T_s^3$ that is disabled in s. Since t is in T_s^2, we know $active(t) \subseteq P$. Two cases are possible. If there exists a process $P_i \in active(t)$ such that $s(i) \neq (pre(t) \cap P_i)$, one can choose process P_i in step 2.a.i of Algorithm 3 and include all transitions t' such that $(pre(t) \cap P_i) \in post(t')$. Consider such a transition t'. If $s(i) \in pre(t')$, t' is in T_s^2 since $P_i \in P$ (and also in T_s^3, since $t' \in T_s$). Else, t' is disabled in s (process P_i, which is active for t', is not ready to execute t') and is neither in T_s^2, nor in T_s^3. By applying repeatedly step 2.a.i of Algorithm 3 and choosing P_i, a transition t'' in T_s^2 may eventually be included in set T_s. In this case, intermediate transitions t''' that are included in set T_s during these successive applications of step 2.a.i are all disabled in s, since they are not in T_s^2 (by construction), and hence process P_i, which is active for all these transitions, is not ready to execute any of them: $s(i) \notin pre(t''')$. Since t'' is in both T_s and T_s^2, it is also in T_s^3.

Now consider the second possible case where, for all processes P_i active for t, we have $s(i) = (pre(t) \cap P_i)$. Since t is disabled in s, there exists a condition c_j in the guard G of t that evaluates to false in s. Such a condition c_j is chosen in step 2.a.ii of Algorithm 3, and all transitions t' such that $\exists op' \in used(t')$: op and op' can-be-dependent, where op is an operation used by t to evaluate c_j, are added to T_s. Consider such a transition t'. If t and t' are parallel, by step 2.b of Algorithm 2, all processes in $active(t')$ are in P. If there is a process P_j such that $s(j) \in pre(t')$, t' is in T_s^2 (and in T_s^3). If for all processes P_j in $active(t')$, $s(j) \notin pre(t')$, t' is disabled in s and is neither in T_s^2, nor in T_s^3. Let P_j be one of the processes active for t'. By applying repeatedly step 2.a.i of Algorithm 3 and choosing P_j, a transition t'' in T_s^2 may eventually be included in set T_s. In this case, intermediate transitions t''' that are included in set T_s during these successive applications of step 2.a.i are all disabled in s, since they are not in T_s^2 (by construction), and hence process P_j, which is active for all these transitions, is not ready to execute any of them: $s(j) \notin pre(t''')$. Since t'' is in both T_s and T_s^2, it is also in T_s^3.

Finally, if t and t' are not parallel, there exists a process P_j active for both t and t'. If $s(j) \in pre(t')$, t' is in T_s^2, and then is also in T_s^3. Else, by applying repeatedly step 2.a.i of Algorithm 3 and choosing P_j, a transition t'' in T_s^2 may eventually be included in set T_s. In this case, intermediate transitions t''' that are included in set T_s during these successive applications of step 2.a.i are all disabled in s, since they are not in T_s^2 (by construction), and hence process P_j, which is active for all these transitions, is not ready to execute any of them: $s(j) \notin pre(t''')$. Since t'' is in both T_s and T_s^2, it is also in T_s^3.

In conclusion, we have build a set T_s^3 such that, for all transitions $t \in T_s^2$, if $t \in T_s^3$, then all enabled transitions that are added to T_s^3 because of t by (possibly several applications of) step 2 of Algorithm 3 are in T_s^2. Consequently, there exists an execution of Algorithm 3 that returns a persistent set $Algo_3(t)$ such that $Algo_3(t) \subseteq Algo_2(t)$. ∎

It follows from the two previous theorems that the smallest persistent set that can be computed by Algorithm i can also be computed by Algorithm j with $i < j$, while the converse is not true, as it has been shown with the examples in the previous Sections.

So far, we have presented three different algorithms, which have been developed independently, and we have shown that they all compute persistent sets. Persistent sets are thus a key notion underlying these algorithms though, maybe surprisingly, none of [Ove81, GW91b, Val91] pointed this out.

It should be emphasized that persistent sets are really *what* we want to compute, while the algorithms that we have presented (including the notion of stubborn sets) rather tell us *how* to compute persistent sets. Making this distinction between "what" and "how" is important. Indeed, once one clearly knows what one wants to obtain, i.e., persistent sets, it is then possible to consider the problem of computing persistent sets from a broader perspective. More precisely, it now makes sense to ask if there exist better algorithms that could compute yet smaller persistent sets than the most elaborate technique we have presented so far, i.e., the stubborn set technique.

The answer to this question is positive, and a new more refined algorithm to compute smaller persistent sets is introduced in the next Section. (The key contributions of the next Section appeared in [GP93].)

4.7   Algorithm 4 (Conditional Stubborn Sets)

4.7.1   Basic Idea

The only information about the current state that has been used in all the previous algorithms for computing persistent sets is whether transitions are enabled or disabled in that state. These algorithms did not use any other information about the current state itself. Indeed, definitions like "can-be-dependent" or "do-not-accord" used by these algorithms were defined with respect to all possible states in S. Therefore, using these definitions can produce unnecessarily large persistent sets.

In this Section, we show how to improve the previous algorithms by using a less restrictive approach. This approach consists in considering only the states *that are reachable from the current state s* and in taking advantage of *conditional dependency*.

We now give a new definition inspired by the stubborn set definition 4.15 that can be used to compute smaller persistent sets. Unlike Definition 4.15, the new definition takes advantage of conditional dependency [GP93].

Definition 4.22 A set T_s of transitions is a *conditional stubborn set* in state s if T_s contains at least one enabled transition, and if for all transitions $t \in T_s$, the following condition holds:

> for all sequences $s = s_1 \xrightarrow{t_1} s_2 \xrightarrow{t_2} s_3 \ldots \xrightarrow{t_{n-1}} s_n \xrightarrow{t_n} s_{n+1}$ of transitions from s in A_G such that t and t_n are dependent in s_n, at least one of the $t_1, \ldots, t_n$ is also in T_s.

∎

Like Definition 4.15, Definition 4.22 defines sets T_s containing transitions that can be either enabled or disabled in s. However, the new definition does not consider all states in S, but only successor states of s in A_G. Moreover, it does not distinguish enabled from disabled transitions: it requires the same condition for all transitions in T_s. Finally, note that this definition is general, abstract, in the sense that it is independent of any particular model.

Let T be the set of all transitions in a conditional stubborn set T_s that are enabled in s. By definition of T_s, T is nonempty. We now prove that T is a persistent set in s.

Theorem 4.23 *Let T be the set of all transitions in a conditional stubborn set T_s in state s that are enabled in s. Then, T is a persistent set in s.*

Proof:

The proof is by contradiction. Suppose that T is not persistent in s. Then, by Definition 4.1, there exists in A_G a sequence $s = s_1 \xrightarrow{t_1} s_2 \xrightarrow{t_2} s_3 \ldots \xrightarrow{t_{n-1}} s_n \xrightarrow{t_n} s_{n+1}$ of transitions $t_1, t_2, \ldots, t_n \notin T$, such that t_n is dependent in s_n with some transition $t \in T$. Let us show that such a sequence cannot exist.

Since $t \in T$, we have $t \in T_s$ and t is enabled in s. Hence, by applying the definition of a conditional stubborn set to t with the sequence $s = s_1 \xrightarrow{t_1} s_2 \xrightarrow{t_2} s_3 \ldots \xrightarrow{t_{n-1}} s_n \xrightarrow{t_n} s_{n+1}$ given above, at least one of the $t_1, \ldots, t_n$ is also in T_s. Let t_i be this transition: $t_i \in T_s$. If t_i is enabled in s, then $t_i \in T$, which contradicts the assumption that $t_1, \ldots, t_n \notin T$. Thus, t_i is disabled in s. Since t_i is enabled in s_i, by applying the definition of a conditional stubborn set to $t_i \in T_s$ with the sequence $s = s_1 \xrightarrow{t_1} s_2 \xrightarrow{t_2} s_3 \ldots \xrightarrow{t_{i-1}} s_i$, at least one of the transitions $t_1, \ldots, t_{i-1}$ is also in T_s. Let t_j, $j < i$, be this transition: $t_j \in T_s$. Again, if t_j is enabled in s, then $t_j \in T$, which contradicts the assumption that $t_1, \ldots, t_n \notin T$. Thus, t_j is disabled in s. By repeating the same reasoning, one comes to the conclusion that t_1 is in T_s. Since t_1 is enabled in s, this means that $t_1 \in T$, which contradicts the assumption that $t_1, \ldots, t_n \notin T$. ∎

It is worth noticing that the converse also holds: for a given state s, every persistent set in s is the set of enabled transitions in a conditional stubborn set in s.

Theorem 4.24 *Let T be a nonempty persistent set in s. Then, there exists a conditional stubborn set T_s in s such that T is the set of all the transitions that are enabled in T_s.*

Proof:

Simply take $T_s = T$. Since T is persistent in s, we know from Definition 4.1 that for all transitions $t \notin T$ such that there exists in A_G a sequence $s = s_1 \xrightarrow{t_1} s_2 \xrightarrow{t_2} s_3 \ldots \xrightarrow{t_{n-1}} s_n \xrightarrow{t_n = t} s_{n+1}$ leading from s to t and including only transitions $t_i \notin T$, t is independent in s_n with all transitions in T. Thus, according to Definition 4.22, no other transition needs be added in T_s, and T itself is a conditional stubborn set. ∎

Consequently, *all* persistent sets can be obtained by computing conditional stubborn sets.

It can also be proved that all stubborn sets are conditional stubborn sets, while the converse does not hold.

Theorem 4.25 *Let T_s be a stubborn set in state s. Then, T_s is also a conditional stubborn set in s.*

Proof:

Consider a transition $t \in T_s$ that is disabled in s. The first transitions t_n that are dependent with t in some state s_n reachable from s in A_G are transitions such that $s_n \xrightarrow{t_n} s_{n+1}$, t is disabled in s_n and t is enabled in s_{n+1}. By Definition 4.14, for all sequences w of transitions from s to such a state s_n, w contains at least one transition in each set $NES(t, s)$. Since all transitions in one set $NES(t, s)$ are in T_S by point 1 of Definition 4.15, all transitions in T_s that are disabled in s satisfy the condition given in Definition 4.22.

Consider a transition $t \in T_s$ that is enabled in s. In all states s_n reachable from s in A_G where the first transitions t_n that are dependent with t are enabled, t is also enabled. Since t and t_n are simultaneously enabled in s_n and are dependent in s_n, they do-not-accord with each other, and all such transitions t_n are in T_s by point 2 of Definition 4.15. Hence, all transitions in T_s that are enabled in s satisfy the condition given in Definition 4.22. ∎

4.7.2   Algorithm

In other words, Definition 4.22 is finer than Definition 4.15 and can be used to produce smaller persistent sets, and actually, all persistent sets in s.

This is a strong, though purely theoretical, result. Indeed, it is not obvious how to develop a practical algorithm that would be able to take advantage of Definition 4.22, since this definition uses information about sequences of transitions in the state space A_G, about which no assumption can be made.

Nevertheless, this more general definition can be profitably used to justify the correctness of a new relation which models more finely the possible interactions between operations on a given object. More precisely, our idea is to define a relation between operations on a given object that would tell us for each operation op used by a transition in T_s which other operations op' "might be the first to interfere with op from the current state s", and thus which other transitions should be added to T_s

as well. The relation "might be the first to interfere with op from the current state s" is represented by the relation $\rhd_s$, which is formally defined as follows.

Definition 4.26 Let op and op' be two operations on the same object O and s be a reachable state. The relation $op \rhd_s op'$ holds if there exists a sequence $s = s_1 \xrightarrow{t_1} s_2 \xrightarrow{t_2} s_3 \ldots \xrightarrow{t_{n-1}} s_n \xrightarrow{t_n} s_{n+1}$ of transitions from s in A_G such that $\forall 1 \leq i < n : \forall op''$ on O used by t_i: op and op'' are independent in state s_i, t_n uses op', and op and op' are dependent in s_n. ∎

The difference between the relation $\rhd_s$ and the relations "can-be-dependent" (Definition 4.6) and "do-not-accord" (Definition 4.13) is that dependencies between transitions are only considered in successor states of s in A_G, not for all states in S, and that only the first dependent operations that may occur from s are considered, instead of all dependent operations.

For any state s, the relation $\rhd_s$ is included in the relation "can-be-dependent" (Definition 4.6): two operations op and op' that satisfy the condition given in the definition of $\rhd_s$ satisfy the condition given in the definition of relation "can-be-dependent", while the converse does not hold, since all paths from the current state s to states where op and op' are dependent may contain a transition from some intermediate state s' that uses an operation op'' dependent with op in s'.

For any state s, the relation $\rhd_s$ is also included in the relation "do-not-accord" (Definition 4.13). Indeed, if op and op' satisfy the condition given in the definition of $\rhd_s$, then there exists a sequence $s = s_1 \xrightarrow{t_1} s_2 \xrightarrow{t_2} s_3 \ldots \xrightarrow{t_{n-1}} s_n \xrightarrow{t_n} s_{n+1}$ of transitions from s in A_G such that $\forall 1 \leq i < n : \forall op''$ on O used by t_i: op and op'' are independent in state s_i, t_n uses op', and op and op' are dependent in s_n. Therefore, op remains defined in all states s_i, $1 \leq i \leq n$, and since op and op' are dependent in s_n and both defined in s_n, they do-not-accord. The converse is not true, since all paths from the current state s to states where op and op' are both defined and dependent may contain a transition from some intermediate state s' that uses an operation op'' dependent with op in s'.

This proves that the relation $\rhd_s$ models the possible interactions between operations on a given object more finely than the relations "can-be-dependent" and "do-not-accord".

Moreover, it can be proved that this relation can profitably replace the two latter relations in *all the previous algorithms* for computing persistent sets, i.e., Algorithms 1, 2 and 3, while still producing persistent sets. Here, we will only prove this result for Algorithm 3, the most elaborate algorithm considered so far, in order to

1. Take one transition t that is enabled in s. Let $T_s = \{t\}$.

2. For all transitions t in T_s:

   (a) if t is disabled in s, either:

      i. choose a process $P_j \in active(t)$ such that $s(j) \neq (pre(t) \cap P_j)$; then, add to T_s all transitions t' such that $(pre(t) \cap P_j) \in post(t')$.

      ii. choose a condition c_j in the guard G of t that evaluates to false in s; then, for all operations op used by t to evaluate c_j, add to T_s all transitions t' such that $\exists op' \in used(t') : op \rhd_s op'$.

   (b) if t is enabled in s, add to T_s all transitions t' such that

      i. t and t' are in conflict; or

      ii. t and t' are parallel and $\exists op \in used(t), \exists op' \in used(t') : op \rhd_s op'$.

3. Repeat step 2 until no more transitions need be added. Then, return all transitions in T_s that are enabled in s (transitions in T_s that are disabled in s are discarded).

Figure 4.5: Algorithm 4

clearly establish that the new technique extends previous work. (The extension of Algorithm 1 and 2 can be done in a similar way.)

Assume that a $\rhd_s$ relation is given for all operations that can be performed on shared objects. (We will discuss later how to provide $\rhd_s$ in practice.) Then, consider Algorithm 3 again, and replace the relations "can-be-dependent" and "do-not-accord" by $\rhd_s$. We obtain Algorithm 4, presented in Figure 4.5. Note that $\rhd_s$ is used in both steps 2.a and 2.b.

We first prove that Algorithm 4 returns persistent sets in s. For doing this, by Theorem 4.23, it is sufficient to show that the sets T_s that it computes are conditional stubborn sets in s.

Theorem 4.27 *All sets T_s that are computed by Algorithm 4 are conditional stubborn sets in s.*

Proof:

Let T_s be a set of transitions that is computed by Algorithm 4. Let us show that T_s is a conditional stubborn set in s.

Consider a transition $t \in T_s$ that is disabled in s. The first transitions t_n that are dependent with t in some state s_n reachable from s in A_G by a sequence w of transitions are transitions such that $s_n \xrightarrow{t_n} s_{n+1}$, t is disabled in s_n, and t is enabled in s_{n+1}. Consider such a sequence w of transitions from s in A_G: $s = s_1 \xrightarrow{t_1} s_2 \xrightarrow{t_2} s_3 \ldots \xrightarrow{t_{n-1}} s_n \xrightarrow{t_n} s_{n+1}$. Two cases are possible in step 2.a: either a process $P_i \in active(t)$ such that $s(i) \neq (pre(t) \cap P_i)$ is chosen, or a condition c_i in the guard G of transition t that evaluates to false in s is chosen by Algorithm 4. In the first case, since t is enabled in s_{n+1}, $s_{n+1}(i) = (pre(t) \cap P_i)$, and thus there exists a transition t_j, $1 \leq j \leq n$, such that $(pre(t) \cap P_k) \in post(t_j)$, which is hence included in set T_s by step 2.a.i. of Algorithm 4. In the second case, there exists a transition t_j, $1 \leq j \leq n$, such that t_j changes the value of c_i from false to true by modifying the output returned by an operation op used to evaluate c_i, i.e., by performing an operation dependent with op in s_j. If there are several such transitions, let t_j be the first transition in w that uses an operation op' dependent with op in s_j. By definition of $\triangleright_s$, we have $op \triangleright_s op'$, and thus t_j is in T_s by step 2.a.ii. This proves that all disabled transitions in T_s satisfy point 1 of Definition 4.22.

Consider a transition $t \in T_s$ that is enabled in s. In all states s_n reachable from s in A_G by a sequence w of transitions where the first transitions t_n that are dependent with t are enabled, t is also enabled. Consider such a sequence w of transitions from s in A_G: $s = s_1 \xrightarrow{t_1} s_2 \xrightarrow{t_2} s_3 \ldots \xrightarrow{t_{n-1}} s_n \xrightarrow{t_n} s_{n+1}$. We thus have that t and t_n are enabled in s_n and are dependent in s_n. If t and t' are not parallel, this implies by Definition 4.5 that at least one process is active for both transitions t and t_n: $P_i \in (active(t) \cap active(t_n))$. If t and t_n are in conflict, t_n is added to T_s by step 2.b.i. If t and t_n are not in conflict, we know that $(pre(t) \cap pre(t_n)) = \emptyset$. Therefore, $(pre(t) \cap P_i) \neq (pre(t_n) \cap P_i)$, and it is impossible for t and t_n to be simultaneously enabled (process P_i cannot be in two different local states $(pre(t) \cap P_i)$ and $(pre(t') \cap P_i)$ at the same time), which contradicts the assumption that t and t_n are both enabled in s_n.

Assume now that t and t' are parallel. We know from Definition 3.21 that a sufficient syntactic condition for two transitions t and t_n to be independent in a state s_n is that they are parallel and $\forall op_1 \in used(t)$ and $\forall op_2 \in used(t_n)$, if op_1 and op_2 are two operations on a same object, then op_1 and op_2 are independent in s_n. Since t and t_n are dependent in s', this implies that $\exists op \in used(t)$, $\exists op' \in used(t_n)$: op and op' are dependent in s'. Let t_j, $1 \leq j \leq n$ be the first transition in w that uses an operation op'' dependent (in s_j) with the operation op used by t. By definition of $\triangleright_s$, we have $op \triangleright_s op''$. Hence, by step 2.b.ii of Algorithm 4, t_j is included in T_s. This proves that all enabled transitions in T_s satisfy point 2 of Definition 4.22. ∎

For a given state s, let $Algo_i(t)$ denote a persistent set that is returned by Algorithm i, with $i \in \{3, 4\}$, when t is the enabled transition chosen in step 1 of the algorithm. Let us now compare the possible persistent sets that can be computed by Algorithm 3 and 4.

Theorem 4.28 *For all transitions t that are enabled in a state s, for all persistent sets $Algo_3(t)$ that can be returned by Algorithm 3, there exists an execution of Algorithm 4 that returns a persistent set $Algo_4(t)$ such that $Algo_4(t) \subseteq Algo_3(t)$.*

Proof:

Immediate by the definition of $\triangleright_s$, since relation $\triangleright_s$ is included in both relations "can-be-dependent" and "do-not-accord". Indeed, since the only difference between Algorithm 3 and 4 is the replacement of the relations "can-be-dependent" and "do-not-accord" by a finer relation $\triangleright_s$, the set T_s constructed by Algorithm 4 is always a subset (not necessarily proper) of the set T_s constructed by Algorithm 3, provided that the same choices are made in case of nondeterminism. ∎

To use Algorithm 4 in practice, we finally have to determine for each type of shared object what the relation $\triangleright_s$ is for each pair (op, op') of possible operations on this object. Like all the other relations on operations we have defined so far (dependency, "can-be-dependent", "do-not-accord"), $\triangleright_s$ can only be approximated in practice, by using sufficient conditions that ensure that "enough" operations are considered. In other words, we have by default $op \triangleright_s op'$ unless it can be proved that it is impossible to have a sequence of transitions in A_G satisfying Definition 4.26. (Note that the relation $\triangleright_s$ can always be approximated by using a relation "can-be-dependent" or "do-not-accord", since these two relations include relation $\triangleright_s$.)

Example 4.29 The following table represents a possible relation $\triangleright_s$ for the bounded FIFO channel of size N considered in Example 3.20. For two operations op and op' on a same channel, if the condition given in row op and column op' in the table is true in a state s, then we have $op \triangleright_s op'$, while "–" denotes the fact that $op \not\triangleright_s op'$.

$\triangleright_s$	Send	Receive	Length	Empty	Full
Send	$n < N$	$n = N$	$n < N$	$n < N$	$n = N - 1$
Receive	$n = 0$	$n > 0$	$n > 0$	$n = 1$	$n > 0$
Length	$n < N$	$n > 0$	–	–	–
Empty	$n = 0$	$n > 0$	–	–	–
Full	$n < N$	$n = N$	–	–	–

For instance, let us show how to determine when $Send \triangleright_s Receive$. One has to determine when it is impossible to find a sequence $s = s_1 \xrightarrow{t_1} s_2 \xrightarrow{t_2} s_3 \ldots \xrightarrow{t_{m-1}} s_m \xrightarrow{t_m} s_{m+1}$ of transitions from s in A_G such that the $Send$ and $Receive$ operations are dependent in s_m, and $\forall 1 \leq i < m : \forall op''$ used by t_i: $Send$ and op'' are independent in state s_i. Since $Send$ and $Receive$ are dependent in s_m, we obtain from the conditional dependency relation between $Send$ and $Receive$ (see the table given in Example 3.20) that either $n = 0$ or $n = N$ in s_m. If $n = 0$ in s_m, the $Receive$ operation is not defined in s_m and there cannot be a transition t_m executing a $Receive$ operation such that $s_m \xrightarrow{t_m} s_{m+1}$. If $n = N$ in s_m, the $Receive$ operation is defined. If $n < N$ in s, and since $n = N$ in s_m, at least one transition t_i, $1 \leq i < m$, in the sequence from s to s_m executes an operation that changes the value of n from $n < N$ to N. This operation can only be a $Send$ operation and is performed from state s_i where $n < N$. Therefore, we obtain from the conditional dependency relation between $Send$ and $Send$ when $n < N$ that the two $Send$ operations are dependent in s_i. It is thus impossible to find a sequence satisfying Definition 4.26 when $n < N$ in s. One concludes that $Send \triangleright_s Receive$ only when $n = N$ in s. ∎

Note that it would not have been possible to obtain such a proof without using conditional dependency and conditional stubborn sets. Also note that relation $\triangleright_s$ is not necessarily symmetric.

Example 4.30 Consider a system containing two processes $A = \{a_0, a_1\}$ and $B = \{b_0, b_1, b_2, b_3\}$, an object of type "bounded FIFO channel" of size $N = 5$, denoted q, as considered in Examples 3.20 and 4.29, an object x of type "boolean variable", and five transitions

$$
\begin{aligned}
&t_1 = (a_0, true, Receive(q), a_1), \quad &&t_3 = (b_0, true, x := 1, b_1), \\
&t_2 = (a_1, true, x := 0, a_0), \quad &&t_4 = (b_1, Empty(q), skip, b_2), \\
& && t_5 = (b_1, Not(Empty(q)), skip, b_3),
\end{aligned}
$$

where it is assumed that $Receive(q)$ denotes a command that performs a $Receive$ operation on the object q (the output of the $Receive$ operation on q is discarded here), $Empty(q)$ denotes a boolean condition equivalent to the value returned by the execution of an $Empty$ operation on object q, and $skip$ denotes some internal (purely local) computation. Consider the state $s = (a_0, b_0, (m_1, m_2, m_3), 0) \in A \times B \times V_q \times V_x$ (q contains the sequence of three messages $m_1 m_2 m_3$). In state s, both transitions t_1 and t_3 are enabled. As an exercice, the reader can compute what the persistent sets that can be returned by Algorithms 1, 2 and 3 are. Actually, $Algo_1(t_1) = $

$Algo_1(t_3) = Algo_2(t_1) = Algo_2(t_3) = Algo_3(t_1) = Algo_3(t_3) = \{t_1, t_3\}$. In other words, neither Algorithm 1, nor Algorithm 2, nor Algorithm 3 is able to return a nontrivial persistent set for this example. Let us investigate how Algorithm 4, in contrast, is able to determine that $\{t_1\}$ is a persistent set in s. Starting with t_1 as the initial enabled transition taken in step 1, Algorithm 4 has to include in set T_s transitions that satisfy either point 2.b.i or point 2.b.ii. Since no transition is in conflict with t_1, no transition is included by step 2.b.i. Since the only operation used by t_1 is a *Receive* operation on q, and since $n = 3$ in s (there are three messages in q), the relation $\rhd_s$ for q given in Example 4.29 tells us to include by point 2.b.ii all transitions that use either a *Receive*, a *Length*, or a *Full* operation on q. Since there is no such transition other than t_1 itself, no other transition is included in T_s. (Note that Algorithm 3 would have included transition t_4 and t_5 by step 2.b.ii of Algorithm 3, since a *Receive* operation and an *Empty* operation do-not-accord with each other (when $n = 1$, they are both defined and are dependent).) Hence, $Algo_4(t_1) = \{t_1\}$, and a persistent-set selective search using Algorithm 4 may only execute transition t_1 from state s. ∎

4.8   Discussion

Four algorithms for computing persistent sets have been presented. These algorithms follow the same general algorithmic idea: they start by taking an enabled transition and then compute a persistent set from this transition by adding repeatedly all transitions that might interfere with it. They can all be viewed as approximations of conditional stubborn sets (cf. Definition 4.22) introduced in the previous Section. Note that other algorithms approximating Definition 4.22 are also possible.

We showed that

- $Algo_1(t) \supseteq Algo_2(t)$,

- $\exists Algo_3(t) : Algo_2(t) \supseteq Algo_3(t)$, and

- $\forall Algo_3(t), \exists Algo_4(t) : Algo_3(t) \supseteq Algo_4(t)$.

For the first three algorithms, we also showed that the worst-case time complexity to compute $Algo_1(t)$, $Algo_2(t)$, and $Algo_3(t)$ are, respectively, $O(|enabled(s)|^2)$, $O(|\mathcal{P}|^2)$, and $O(|\mathcal{T}|^2)$. Clearly, the more information about the system description the algorithm uses and can exploit, the more sophisticated the algorithm is, the smaller the persistent set that it returns can be, but the larger the run-time is.

There is an exception to this rule: the worst-case time complexity to compute $Algo_4(t)$ is the same as the one of $Algo_3(t)$. Indeed, the only difference between Algorithm 3 and Algorithm 4 is that Algorithm 4 takes advantage of the relation $\triangleright_s$, which models more finely the possible interactions between operations on shared objects. In other words, Algorithm 4 improves Algorithm 3 while preserving the same time complexity. Actually, the relations "can-be-dependent" and "do-not-accord" should be replaced by the relation $\triangleright_s$ in all the algorithms presented in this chapter, i.e., Algorithms 1, 2 and 3: *this is a no-risk and free improvement.*

Of course, a relation $\triangleright_s$ has to be provided for each type of shared objects. But, in practice, interactions between operations on shared objects have to be described somehow anyway. We have showed that the relation $\triangleright_s$ gives the most general existing framework for modeling interactions between operations, extending the relations "can-be-dependent" and "do-not-accord". In practice, it is worth defining $\triangleright_s$ as finely as possible, in order to improve the effectiveness of the algorithms described in this chapter. Note that this has to be done only once for each type of shared object.

Therefore, we advocate the use of object libraries where classic high-level communication objects (such as various definitions of communication channels, shared variables, semaphores, etc), operations on these objects, the dependency and $\triangleright_s$ relations are defined as carefully as possible once for all. One can then specify concurrent systems by using these object libraries and thus gain from the refined dependencies during verification which is still fully automatic. In contrast, we discourage the opposite approach consisting of defining only one type "shared variable", which can be used to represent any shared object, or even worst, the approach consisting in defining "everything", including objects, by processes (for instance, a transmission medium can be modeled by a process that transmits messages). Note that this recommendation is quite natural. Indeed, when using such specialized objects, one indirectly provides more information to the verification tool about the structure of the state space of the system being analyzed. If the tool is clever enough to be able to use this information (as is the case with a "partial-order" verification tool), it is not surprising that the verification can be performed more efficiently and becomes applicable to larger systems.

Another question is: which algorithm among Algorithms 1, 2, and 3 should be used in conjunction with a relation $\triangleright_s$? It is difficult to answer this question.

Indeed, on one hand, it is easy to see that if a persistent set T in a state s is a subset of another persistent set T' in s, then the reduced state-space A_R obtained by choosing T in state s is smaller than the reduced state-space A'_R obtained by choosing

T' in state s (provided that the same rule is applied in all other visited states of A_R). Therefore, T should be prefered to T'.

However, on the other hand, if a persistent set T in a state s contains less transitions than another persistent set T' in s, but is not a subset of T', then choosing T instead of T' is just a heuristics: the reduced state-space A_R obtained by choosing T in s will not necessarily be smaller than the reduced state-space A'_R obtained by choosing T' in s.

This implies that there is no "best" algorithm for computing persistent sets. Indeed, $min(PS_j)$, the smallest persistent set that can be computed by Algorithm j, is not necessarily included in $min(PS_i)$, $i < j$. Computing as small persistent sets as possible is only a heuristics. Moreover, computing smaller persistent sets can only be done at an additional run-time expense, and using a more elaborate algorithm does not systematically yield smaller persistent sets: an elaborate algorithm may return the same persistent set as a simple algorithm, it then requires more time to produce the same result.

Therefore, in practice, the choice of a persistent-set algorithm is a trade-off between the complexity of the algorithm, its additional run-time expense, and the reduction it can yield. This choice also depends on the model used to represent concurrent systems (some information is hard to extract from some models), and on the type of systems that have to be analyzed (some optimizations are useless for some classes of examples).

Note 4.31 In [Val91], it is pointed out that all transitions that can disable an enabled transition in a stubborn set T_s need not systematically be included in T_s, if at least one enabled transition in T_s is independent with all transitions not in T_s. From this observation, Valmari introduced another variant of stubborn sets, called "weak stubborn sets" [Val91]. Note that, following the idea of Valmari, "weak" versions of our notions of persistent set and of conditional stubborn set can easily be defined. ■

Note 4.32 A definition very similar to our definition of persistent set appeared (independently) in [KP92b]. This definition is the following.

> Let s be a state. A *faithful decomposition in* s is a subset of transitions $T_s \subseteq T$ such that each transition in $T \setminus T_s$ is either independent of each transition in T_s or is disabled in s and its successors as long as no operation of T_s is executed.

It is easy to see that the set of all enabled transitions in a faithful decomposition T_s in s is persistent in s. ∎

Chapter 5

Sleep Sets

5.1   Basic Idea

The second technique for computing the set of transitions T to consider in a selective search is the *sleep set* technique [GW93] introduced in [God90]. This technique does not exploit information about the static structure (code) of the program, as persistent-set algorithms do, but rather information about the past of the search. Used in conjunction with a persistent-set technique, sleep sets can further reduce the number of states explored. Indeed, when the persistent-set technique cannot avoid the selection of *independent* transitions in a state, sleep sets can avoid the wasteful exploration of multiple interleavings of these transitions.

Example 5.1 Consider a system containing two processes $A = \{a_0, a_1, a_2\}$ and $B = \{b_0, b_1, b_2\}$, two objects x and y of type "boolean variable", and four transitions

$$t_1 = (a_0, true, x := 0, a_1), \quad t_3 = (b_0, true, y := 1, b_1),$$
$$t_2 = (a_1, true, y := 0, a_2), \quad t_4 = (b_1, true, x := 1, b_2).$$

Consider the state $s = (a_0, b_0, 0, 0) \in A \times B \times V_x \times V_y$. In state s, both transitions t_1 and t_3 are enabled. The global state space A_G corresponding to this system is shown in Figure 5.1. It is easy to see that the only persistent set in s is the set $\{t_1, t_3\}$ of all enabled transitions. Therefore, every persistent-set selective search, whatever algorithm it uses to compute persistent sets, has to execute both transitions t_1 and t_3 from state s. Note that transitions t_1 and t_3 are independent in s. ∎

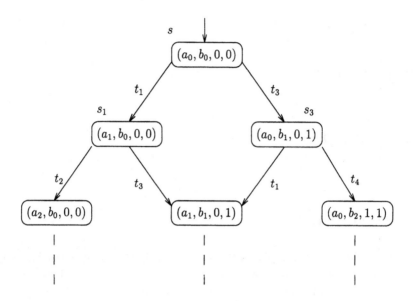

Figure 5.1: Global state space for the system of Example 5.1

Let us consider an example to illustrate the basic idea behind sleep sets. Consider again the system of Example 5.1. In state s, two enabled independent transitions t_1 and t_3 are selected to be explored from s. After exploring t_1, t_3 is still enabled since t_1 and t_3 are independent in s, and t_3 could thus be selected to be explored from the state s_1 reached after executing t_1 from s. Conversely, after exploring t_3, t_1 will, for the same reason, also still be enabled and could also be selected to be explored from the state s_3 reached after executing t_3 from s. When selecting two independent transitions t_1 and t_3 from s, there is thus a risk that the two interleavings of t_1 and t_3, i.e., the two sequences $t_1 t_3$ and $t_3 t_1$, will be explored. This is potentially wasteful since both of these interleavings lead to the same state. In order to prevent this situation from occurring, the sleep set method prevents the exploration of t_1 in s_3: t_1 is introduced in the "sleep set associated with s_3".

More precisely, a *sleep set* is a set of transitions. A sleep set is associated with each state s reached during the search. The sleep set associated with a state s is a set of transitions that are *enabled* in s but *will not be executed* from s. The sleep set associated with the initial state s_0 is the empty set. The sleep sets of the successors of a state s are then computed as follows.

Let T be the set of transitions that have been selected to be explored from s, and let $s.Sleep$ denote the sleep set associated with s. Take a first transition t_1 out of T. The sleep set associated with the state reached after executing t_1 from s is the sleep set associated with s unmodified except for the elimination of the transitions that are dependent with t_1 in s. (Equivalently, only the transitions of the sleep set associated with s that are independent with t_1 in s are passed to the sleep set associated with the state reached after executing t_1 from s.) Let t_2 be a second transition taken out of T. The sleep set associated with the state reached after executing t_2 from s is the sleep set associated with s augmented with t_1, minus all transitions that are dependent with t_2 in s. One proceeds in a similar way with the remaining transitions of T. The general rule is thus that the sleep set associated with a state s' reached by a transition t from a state s is the sleep set that was obtained when reaching s augmented with all transitions already taken from T, and purged of all transitions that are dependent with t in s.

5.2 Algorithm

The algorithm of Figure 5.2 represents a persistent-set selective search augmented with all operations required to manipulate sleep sets. It uses a *Stack* and a hash table H to store visited states and their associated sleep set. Each time a new state s is encountered during the search (line 6), it is stored in the hash table H, with its associated sleep set $s.Sleep$ (line 7). Then, a call to the function Persistent_Set is performed (line 8). This function returns a persistent set T in s that is nonempty if there exist transitions enabled in s. Transitions that are in the current sleep set $s.Sleep$ need not be explored, and are thus removed from set T (line 8).

If the current state s has already been visited (line 10), let $H(s).Sleep$ denote the sleep set that has been stored with s in H. If $H(s).Sleep$ contains transitions that are not in the current sleep set $s.Sleep$ associated with s, these transitions are selected to be explored (line 11) with a new sleep set equals to $s.Sleep \cap H(s).Sleep$ (lines 12). This new sleep set associated with s is stored with s in the hash table H (line 13). Hence, the value of $H(s).Sleep$ may shrink as the search proceeds, since transitions can be removed from it at a later visit. (Note that $H(s).Sleep$ never grows.)

All transitions selected to be explored, i.e., in set T, are explored (line 15–16), and the sleep set that is to be associated with each successor state of s is computed (line 17–19) following the procedure described above ($s.Sleep$ is used in line 19 as a temporary variable to store all transitions already taken from T during this computation).

```
1      Initialize:Stack is empty; H is empty;
2              s₀.Sleep = ∅;
3              push (s₀) onto Stack;
4      Loop: while Stack ≠ ∅ do {
5              pop (s) from Stack;
6              if s is NOT already in H then {
7                 enter s in H;
8                 T = Persistent_Set(s) \ s.Sleep
9              }
10             else {
11                T = {t | t ∈ H(s).Sleep ∧ t ∉ s.Sleep};
12                s.Sleep = s.Sleep ∩ H(s).Sleep;
13                H(s).Sleep = s.Sleep
14             }
15             for all t in T do {
16                s' = succ(s) after t; /* t is executed */
17                s'.Sleep = {t' ∈ s.Sleep | (t, t') are independent in s };
18                push (s') onto Stack;
19                s.Sleep = s.Sleep ∪ {t}
20             }
21      }
```

Figure 5.2: Selective search using persistent sets and sleep sets

The correctness proof of the algorithm is the following. Let A_R be the reduced state-space explored by the algorithm of Figure 5.2. We now prove that all deadlocks in A_G are in A_R.

Theorem 5.2 *Let s be a state in A_R, and let d be a deadlock reachable from s in A_G by a sequence w of transitions. For all $w_i \in [w]_s$, let t_i denote the first transition of w_i. Let $H(s).Sleep$ denote the sleep set stored with s in H when the search is completed. If for all t_i, t_i is not in $H(s).Sleep$, then d is reachable from s in A_R.*

Proof:

The proof proceeds by induction on the length of w. For $|w| = 0$, the result is immediate. Now, assume the theorem holds for paths (sequences of transitions) of length $n \geq 0$ and let us prove that it holds for a path w of length $n + 1$.

We first prove that at least one of the transitions t_i has been executed from s in A_R. If some of the t_i have been in $H(s).Sleep$ at some moment during the search, they have been removed from $H(s).Sleep$ at a later visit of s, since none of the t_i are in $H(s).Sleep$ when the search is completed; since transitions that are removed from $H(s).Sleep$ are executed, there is at least one of the transitions t_i that has been executed from s in A_R. If none of the t_i were ever in $H(s).Sleep$, this means that none of them were in the sleep set $s.Sleep$ associated with s the very first time it has been visited (since $H(s).Sleep$ can only shrink between successive visits of s). During this first visit, a call to the function Persistent_Set was performed and, from Lemma 4.2, we know that at least one of the t_i was in the persistent set in s that was returned. Since this transition was not in $s.Sleep$, it has been executed from s in A_R.

Now, consider the last visit of s where some of the t_i have been executed from s (we have just proved such a visit exists). Let t_1 denote the first transition t_i that has been explored during this visit. From this visit of s until the end of the search, $H(s).Sleep$ did not contain any transition t_i, since we assumed that $H(s).Sleep$ does not contain any transition t_i at the end of the search, and since none of the t_i are executed from s after this last visit. Let $s.Sleep$ denote the sleep set associated with s just before the execution of t_1 from s. At this moment, $s.Sleep$ does not contain any transition t_i.

Let s' be the state reached after executing t_1 from s. We have $w_1 = t_1 w'$. By Theorem 3.10, since w leads to d in $n + 1$ steps, w_1 also leads to d, in $n + 1$ steps. Consequently, w' leads to d from s', and is of length n. Let us show that, for all $w_i' \in [w']_{s'}$, the first transition t_i' of w_i' is not in $H(s').Sleep$.

Assume the opposite, i.e., there exists some transition $t_i' \in H(s').Sleep$ at the end of the search. Hence, t_i' has always been in $H(s').Sleep$. Consequently, t_i' was in the sleep set $s'.Sleep$ associated with s' when s' was explored from s by t_1. This implies that t_i' and t_1 are independent in s, else t_i' would not have been passed on to $s'.Sleep$. Since they are independent in s, t_i' is enabled in s and is the first transition of a path w_i leading from s to d. Given that t_i' is in $s'.Sleep$, either t_i' was in $s.Sleep$, or t_i' was added after being executed from s. The first possibility is in contradiction with the fact that t_i' is also the first transition of some $w_i \in [w]_s$ leading to d from s and thus is not in $s.Sleep$. The second possibility is incompatible with the fact that t_1, not t_i', is the first transition among the t_i to be executed from s.

The inductive hypothesis can thus be used with w' from s' to establish that d is visited from s' and hence from s. ∎

By applying Theorem 5.2 to the initial state s_0, we directly reach the conclusion that the algorithm of Figure 5.2 indeed reaches all deadlock states, since the sleep set associated to the initial state is the empty set.

The algorithm of Figure 5.2 stores in randomly accessed memory one sleep set $H(s).Sleep$ with each state encountered during the search. The size of $H(s).Sleep$ is bounded by the number of transitions that are enabled in s. Sleep sets $s.Sleep$ associated with states that are in the *Stack* can be stored with these states in a sequentially accessed memory. The overhead in randomly accessed memory due to the use of sleep sets in a persistent-set selective search is thus $O(|S_R||Enabled|)$ where $|S_R|$ denotes the number of states in A_R and $|Enabled|$ is the average number of transitions that are enabled in a state.

Concerning time complexity, each transition in A_R is explored exactly once. Each time a transition t from a state s to a state s' is executed during the search, a sleep set $s'.Sleep$ is computed from $s.Sleep$ and the transitions already taken from s. This can be done in time $O(|enabled(s)|)$ (assuming that it takes $O(1)$ time to check whether two transitions are independent or not in a given state). One also has to check whether s' is already in H: let us assume that this operation takes $O(1)$ time (i.e., that the number of collisions is bounded). When s' has already been visited, $s'.Sleep$ is compared to $H(s').Sleep$: this can be done in $O(|enabled(s')|)$. Overall, the overhead in run time due to the manipulation of sleep sets in a persistent-set selective search is thus $O(|\Delta_R||Enabled|)$ where $|\Delta_R|$ is the number of transitions in A_R and $|Enabled|$ is the average number of transitions that are enabled in a state.

Note 5.3 Obviously, the set $T = \text{Persistent\_Set}(s) \setminus s.Sleep$ of transitions selected to be executed from a state s is, in general, not a persistent set in s. For instance, consider state s_3 in Example 5.1. The sleep set $s_3.Sleep$ associated to state s_3 will be $\{t_1\}$. Since the only persistent set in s_3 is the set $\{t_1, t_4\}$, the set T of transitions executed from s_3 by Algorithm 5.2 will be $\{t_4\}$, which is not persistent in s. This illustrates the fact that sleep sets enable one to go *beyond* persistent sets in computing the transitions that need to be explored in a selective search. ∎

5.3   Properties of Sleep Sets

5.3.1   On Combining Sleep Sets with Persistent Sets

We showed that the notion of sleep set is orthogonal to the notion of persistent set. We also showed how sleep sets and persistent sets can be combined. In this Section, we further discuss this combination.

Consider the case where sleep sets are used alone with a classical search, i.e., without being combined with a persistent-set algorithm. This is equivalent to assume that, in each state s that is visited during the search performed by the algorithm of Figure 5.2, the function Persistent_Set returns the set of all enabled transitions in s. (Since this set is trivially persistent in s, this case is actually a particular case of the general case considered in the previous Section.) Then, we can show that all states in A_G are visited by such a search: all states in A_G are in A_R, where A_R is the reduced state-space explored by such an algorithm.

The proof is based on the following Theorem.

Theorem 5.4 *Let A_R be the reduced state-space explored by the algorithm of Figure 5.2 when the function Persistent_Set always returns the set of all enabled transitions. Let s be a state in A_R, and let x be a state reachable from s in A_G by a sequence w of transitions. For all $w_i \in [w]_s$, let t_i denote the first transition of w_i. Let $H(s).Sleep$ denote the sleep set stored with s in H when the search is completed. If for all t_i, t_i is not in $H(s).Sleep$, then x is reachable from s in A_R.*

Proof:

The proof is similar to the proof of Theorem 5.2. The only difference is that, instead of invoking Lemma 4.2, in the second paragraph of the proof, to deduce that at least one of the t_i leading to the deadlock d is in the set of transitions that is returned by Persistent_Set, the fact that here at least one of the t_i leading to x has been executed from s is straightforward, since all transitions not in $s.Sleep$ are systematically executed from s, including all transitions t_i. ∎

By applying Theorem 5.4 to the initial state s_0, we directly reach the conclusion that the sleep-set algorithm used *without* being combined with a persistent-set algorithm visits *all* reachable states, since the sleep set associated to the initial state is the empty set. In other words, sleep sets used alone cannot reduce the number of states in A_R. However, they can reduce the number of *transitions* in A_R, which can still be very useful (see Chapter 8).

Let us consider another particular case. Assume that, during the search performed by the algorithm of Figure 5.2, the function Persistent_Set never returns enabled transitions *that are independent*. In other words, the function Persistent_Set called in any state s always returns a set T of transitions enabled in s such that, for all t and t' in T, t and t' are dependent in s. In this case, it is easy to see that all sleep sets will always be empty: from the initial state, whose associated sleep set is empty, no transition will ever be introduced in a sleep set, for all successor states. Therefore, the impact of sleep sets will be void, and sleep sets will not yield any reduction in both the number of states and transitions that are explored.

Note that, roughly speaking, using sleep sets with a "perfectly bad" persistent-set algorithm is similar to the first case mentioned above, while using sleep sets with a "perfectly good" persistent-set algorithm might be equivalent to the second case above. In practice, however, persistent-set algorithms are rarely perfectly good or bad in all states, and these two extreme cases rarely occur. Therefore, sleep sets can very often further reduce both the number of states and transitions that need to be explored for verification purposes (see Chapter 8).

5.3.2   Reducing State Matchings

A nice property of sleep sets is that they can strongly decrease the number of state matchings that occur during the search [GHP92]. A state matching occurs each time an already visited state is visited again later during the search. The reduction of state matchings due to sleep sets can be illustrated by the following example.

Example 5.5 Consider a system containing two processes $A = \{a_0, a_1, a_2\}$ and $B = \{b_0, b_1, b_2\}$, two objects x and y of type "boolean variable", and four transitions

$$t_1 = (a_0, true, x := 1, a_1), \quad t_3 = (b_0, true, y := 1, b_1),$$
$$t_2 = (a_1, true, x := 0, a_2), \quad t_4 = (b_1, true, y := 0, b_2).$$

Consider the initial state $s_0 = (a_0, b_0, 0, 0) \in A \times B \times V_x \times V_y$. The reduced state space A_R explored by Algorithm 5.2 for this system when the function Persistent_Set(s) returns the set of all enabled transitions in s is presented in Figure 5.3. The initial state is the state on top of the Figure. The value of the sleep set $H(s).Sleep$ when the search is completed is given between braces beside each state s. Dotted transitions are not explored by the algorithm of Figure 5.2. ∎

For the system considered in the previous example, all states are visited only once by the algorithm of Figure 5.2. Of course, if one could know it in advance before starting the search, it would not be necessary to store *any* states! Unfortunately, for arbitrary systems, it is impossible to determine before the search is completed which are the states that are encountered only once.

We will come back to this property of sleep sets in Chapter 8.

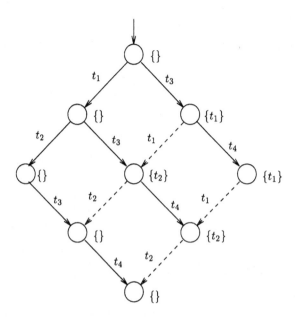

Figure 5.3: Reduced state space with sleep sets

Note 5.6 Another sleep-set algorithm appeared in [GHP92], where two additional assumptions were made: sleep sets were assumed to be used without being combined with a persistent-set algorithm, and the search was assumed to be performed in a "depth-first" order. Under these assumptions, another sleep set algorithm was given, that did not require to store a sleep set $H(s).Sleep$ with each state in H. Note that, in this chapter, no assumptions were made about the order in which the search has to be performed. ■

Chapter 6

Verification of Safety Properties

6.1 Beyond Deadlock Detection

So far, we have presented several selective-search algorithms that explore only a reduced part A_R of the global state space A_G such that all deadlocks in A_G are in A_R. In order to check for properties more elaborate than deadlocks, it is usually necessary to preserve more information, i.e., more states and transitions, in the reduced state space A_R.

Indeed, consider, for instance, the reachability of a *local* state l of a process P_i. Precisely, this problem amounts to checking whether there exists a global state s that is reachable from the initial state s_0 and such that $s(i) = l$. The algorithms presented in the two previous chapters are not sufficient for checking such a property. This is illustrated by the following example.

Example 6.1 Consider a system containing two processes $A = \{a_0, a_1\}$ and $B = \{b_0, l\}$, two objects x and y of type "boolean variable", and three transitions

$$t_1 = (a_0, true, x := 1, a_1), \quad t_3 = (b_0, true, y := 1, l),$$
$$t_2 = (a_1, true, x := 0, a_0).$$

State $s_0 = (a_0, b_0, 0, 0) \in A \times B \times V_x \times V_y$ is the initial state of this system. In s_0, transitions t_1 and t_3 are enabled and independent. The set $\{t_1\}$ is a persistent set in s_0. Hence, a selective search can, for instance, explore only t_1 from s_0. After executing t_1 from s_0, the state $s_1 = (a_1, b_0, 1, 0)$ is reached. In s_1, t_2 and t_3 are enabled and independent, and $\{t_2\}$ is a persistent set in s_1. Thus, a selective search can explore

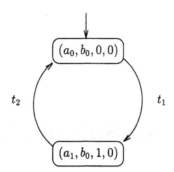

Figure 6.1: Reduced state space for the system of Example 6.1

only t_2 from s_1. After executing t_2, the selective search stops since transition t_2 leads back to the initial state s_0, which has already been visited with an empty sleep set. Transition t_3, though being enabled in s_0 and s_1, has never been explored, and local state l has not been reached. The reduced state space A_R explored, which is shown in Figure 6.1, is sufficient for proving the absence of deadlock in the system: since A can loop forever independently of the rest of the system, i.e., process B, one can conclude that this system is deadlock free even without considering the possible behaviors of B. However, A_R is not sufficient to determine if l is reachable or not from the initial state. ■

The phenomenon illustrated above is referred to as the "ignoring problem" in [Val91]: the behavior of some processes (e.g., B in the above example) can be completely ignored from some state reached during a selective search. In order to check other properties than deadlocks, selective-search algorithms have to be adapted to the type of property one wants to check.

In this chapter, we present a modification of a selective-search algorithm that can be used for checking the reachability of local states, and, more generally, for checking any safety property. The idea is to enforce an additional condition, that we call a *proviso*, during the selective search. This proviso ensures that the choices between enabled independent transitions made during the search are not completely "unfair" with respect to some processes. Our proviso can be used with a selective search that makes use of both persistent sets and sleep sets to select the transitions that are explored.

This chapter is organized as follows. In the next Section, we present the proviso mentioned above. Then, we prove that any selective search using persistent sets and sleep sets augmented with this proviso explores a *trace automaton*. Loosely speaking, a trace automaton for a given system is an automaton that accepts at least one interleaving for each trace (concurrent execution) the system can perform from its initial state. Many interesting properties of a concurrent system can be checked on a trace automaton. These properties are presented in Section 6.4. Finally, we compare our solution with other related work.

6.2   Algorithm

We saw with Example 6.1 that in general, the reduced state space A_R that is explored by a selective-search algorithm using persistent sets and sleep sets, as shown in Figure 5.2, is not sufficient to check the reachability of local states. This problem can be solved by modifying the selective-search algorithm as follows.

The modification consists in enforcing an additional condition, called a *proviso*, on the sets of transitions that are returned by the function Persistent_Set. This proviso requires that the selective search is performed in a depth-first order. Let *Stack* denote the current "depth-first-search stack" during the search, i.e., the set of states that are in the path from the initial state s_0 to the currently visited state. The proviso enforces the following restrictions on the sets of transitions that can be returned by the function Persistent_Set [HGP92].

Definition 6.2 Each time a call to the function Persistent_Set is performed during the search, the persistent set in s that is returned by this function has to satisfy the following requirement:

1. either $\exists t \in$ Persistent_Set(s): $t \notin s.Sleep$ and $s' \notin Stack$, where s' is the successor of s by t ($s \xrightarrow{t} s'$), and $s.Sleep$ is the sleep set associated with s when the call is performed;

2. or Persistent_Set(s) = enabled(s).

∎

In other words, the set Persistent_Set(s) returned by the function Persistent_Set has to contain at least one transition not in the current sleep set $s.Sleep$ and not leading to the current *Stack*. Else, if such a persistent set does not exist, the set of all enabled transitions is returned (remember this set is always a persistent set). Let Persistent_Set_Satisfying_Proviso(s) denote a persistent set in s that satisfies the above proviso.

The algorithm of Figure 6.2 shows how to perform a selective search using persistent sets and sleep sets in a depth-first order. This algorithm is very similar to the one of Figure 5.2. The main difference is that, at any time during the search, the data structure *Stack* now contains exactly the states that are in the path currently being explored from the initial state s_0 to the currently visited state. Note that, as explained in the previous chapter, a state can be visited with different sleep sets, and transitions from this state can be explored at successive visits of the state (though a transition is never explored more than once from the same state). In order to prevent a state s from appearing several times in *Stack* (in case of cycles), and to guarantee that the exploration is performed in a depth-first order, re-explorations of states that are in *Stack* are delayed (line 21–23): the sleep set that has to be associated with s during such a re-exploration is saved in an auxiliary data structure named "*delay*". Later, once s has just been backtracked (line 31), the algorithm checks (line 32) whether there are delayed re-explorations of s. If yes, state s is then re-visited with a sleep set taken out of $delay(s)$ (line 33–35). (The order in which sleep sets are taken out of $delay(s)$ does not matter.)

In what follows, a state s is said to be "visited" when it is accessed from the top of *Stack* in line 8 of the algorithm. s is said to be "backtracked" when it is popped from *Stack* (line 31). When a state s is backtracked, "the last visit of s" is the last time s has been visited, while "during the last visit of s" is the interval of time from the last time s has been visited until the last time it has been backtracked. If $s \xrightarrow{t} s'$, "the sleep set associated with s' after the execution of t from s" denotes the sleep set associated to s' that is computed during the visit of s (line 20) when t is executed from s.

Note that, since the search is performed in a depth-first order, when a state s is backtracked, all the transitions t that have been selected to be executed from s (i.e., that are in set T considered in line 18) during the last visit of s have been executed. Moreover, all the (immediate) successors s' of s by such transitions t that are not in *Stack* have already been visited with the sleep set associated with s' after the execution of t from s, and have already been backtracked. The value of *Stack* just after a state s is visited and just before s is backtracked is the same (and contains s).

Example 6.3 Consider again the system of Example 6.1. A possible reduced state space explored by the algorithm of Figure 6.2 for this system is shown in Figure 6.3.

```
1     Initialize:Stack is empty; H is empty;
2     Search() {
3        s₀.Sleep = ∅; delay(s₀) = ∅;
4        push (s₀) onto Stack;
5        DFS()
6        }
7     DFS() {
8        s = top(Stack); /* s is visited */
9        if s is NOT already in H then {
10          enter s in H;
11          T = Persistent_Set_Satisfying_Proviso(s)\s.Sleep
12          }
13       else {
14          T = {t | t ∈ H(s).Sleep ∧ t ∉ s.Sleep};
15          s.Sleep = s.Sleep ∩ H(s).Sleep;
16          H(s).Sleep = s.Sleep
17          }
18       for all t in T do {
19          s' = succ(s) after t; /* t is executed */
20          s'.Sleep = {t' ∈ s.Sleep | (t,t') are independent in s };
21          if s' is in Stack then {
22             delay(s') = delay (s') ∪ {s'.Sleep}
23             }
24          else {
25             delay(s')= ∅;
26             push (s') onto Stack;
27             DFS()
28             }
29          s.Sleep = s.Sleep ∪ {t}
30          }
31       pop s from Stack; /* s is backtracked */
32       if delay(s)≠ ∅ then {
33          take s.Sleep out of delay(s);
34          push (s) onto Stack;
35          DFS()
36          }
37       }
```

Figure 6.2: Selective search using persistent sets, sleep sets, and proviso

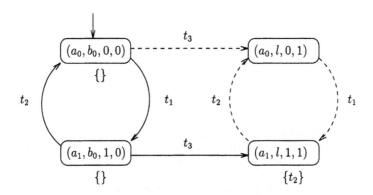

Figure 6.3: Reduced state space with proviso for the system of Example 6.1

The value of the sleep set $H(s).Sleep$ when the search is completed is given between braces below each state s. Dotted transitions are not explored by the algorithm of Figure 6.2. Initially, the persistent set $\{t_1\}$ is selected in the initial state $s_0 = (a_0, b_0, 0, 0)$. State $s_1 = (a_1, b_0, 1, 0)$ is then reached with an empty sleep set. In s_1, $\{t_2\}$ is a persistent set. However, it does not satisfy the proviso since t_2 leads back to the state s_0, which is in *Stack*. Thus, another persistent set has to be computed. The set $\{t_2, t_3\}$ is a persistent set in s_1 and satisfies the proviso since t_3 leads to a state not in *Stack*. By executing t_2 before t_3 in s_1, t_2 is introduced in the sleep set associated to the state $s_2 = (a_1, l, 1, 1)$ reached after the execution of t_3 from s_1. In s_2, only t_2 is enabled. Since it is in the sleep set associated to s_2, it is not executed, and the search stops. Note that, if sleep sets were not used (or if the persistent set $\{t_3\}$ was selected in s_1), t_2 would have been explored from s_2, state $s_3 = (a_0, l, 0, 1)$ would have been explored, and transition t_1 from s_3 would have been explored as well. ■

6.3   Trace Automata

In this Section, we prove that reduced state spaces A_R explored by the algorithm of Figure 6.2 are *trace automata* (introduced in [God90]) provided that the valid conditional dependency relation used is *weakly uniform*.

Intuitively, a trace automaton for a given system is an automaton that accepts at least one interleaving for each trace (concurrent execution) the system can perform from its initial state s_0. Formally, trace automata are defined as follows [God90].

Definition 6.4 Let A_G be the global state space of a system. A reduced state space A_R for this system is a *trace automaton* for this system if, for all sequences w of transitions from the initial state s_0 in A_G, there exists a sequence w' of transitions from s_0 in A_R such that w' is a linearization of a trace defined by an extension of w, i.e., $w \in Pref([w']_{s_0})$, where $Pref([w]_{s_0})$ denotes the set of the prefixes of the sequences in $[w]_{s_0}$. ∎

Let L_{A_G} and L_{A_R} be respectively the languages of finite words formed by symbols of T, i.e., sequences of *transitions*, accepted by the automaton A_G and A_R (cf. Section 2.2). If A_R is a trace automaton for the system, we have:

$$L_{A_G} = \bigcup_{w \in L_{A_R}} Pref([w]_{s_0}).$$

All sequences of transitions from s_0 in A_G are represented by a trace in A_R, hence the name "trace automaton".

Example 6.5 The reduced state space shown in Figure 6.3 is a trace automaton for the system of Example 6.1. Indeed, the reader can check that for all sequences w of transitions from s_0 in A_G, there exists a linearization w' of a trace defined by an extension of w. For instance, consider the sequence $w = t_1 t_2 t_3 t_1 t_2$ from s_0 in A_G. The sequence $w' = t_1 t_2 t_1 t_2 t_1 t_3$ from s_0 in A_R is such that $w'' = t_1 t_2 t_3 t_1 t_2 t_1 \in [w']_{s_0}$ and $w \in Pref(w'')$. ∎

We now prove that the algorithm of Figure 6.2 explores trace automata. However, in order to establish this result, we need to make an additional assumption about the valid conditional dependency relation that is used for computing persistent sets and sleep sets in the algorithm of Figure 6.2: this dependency relation must be *weakly uniform*[1].

Definition 6.6 A valid conditional dependency relation D for a LFCS is said to be *weakly uniform* if $\forall t_1, t_2, t_3 \in T, \forall s \in S$, if we have $s \xrightarrow{t_1} s_1 \xrightarrow{t_2} s_2, s \xrightarrow{t_3} s', (t_1, t_3, s) \notin D$ and $(t_2, t_3, s_1) \notin D$, then $(t_1, t_2, s) \in D$ implies $(t_1, t_2, s') \in D$. ∎

---

[1]by analogy with another, stronger, condition called "uniformity condition", which appeared in [KP92a].

Intuitively, the above definition prevents two transitions that are dependent in some state s and that can be executed one after the other from s to become independent after the execution of a third independent transition. We will see later why this additional assumption is needed.

In a similar way, weakly uniform dependency relations can be defined between operations on objects. It is straightforward to show that the valid conditional dependency relation on transitions obtained with Definition 3.21 and weakly uniform valid conditional dependency relations between operations on objects is weakly uniform. Note that a valid constant dependency relation is trivially weakly uniform.

Example 6.7 The two dependency relations given in Example 3.19 are weakly uniform. In contrast, the dependency relation given in Example 3.20 is not weakly uniform. Indeed, when $n = N - 1$, a *Full* operation can be followed by a *Send* operation on the same bounded FIFO channel of size N, a *Receive* operation is defined and is independent with both *Full* and *Send* operations, *Full* and *Send* operations are dependent, but after executing a *Receive* operation, they become independent (when $n = N - 2$). It is possible to modify the dependency relation given in Example 3.20 to obtain a weakly uniform dependency relation by considering *Send* and *Full* operations as being dependent when $n < N$ (instead of when $n = N - 1$), and *Receive* and *Empty* operations as being dependent when $n > 0$ (instead of when $n = 1$). ■

Let $w = t_1 t_2 \ldots t_n$ be a sequence of transitions from a state s in the global state space A_G of the system being analyzed. Let $s = s_1 \xrightarrow{t_1} s_2 \xrightarrow{t_2} s_3 \ldots \xrightarrow{t_{n-1}} s_n \xrightarrow{t_n} s_{n+1}$ be the sequence of states it goes through. In what follows, "t is independent with all transitions in w" is an abbreviation for "t is independent in s_i with t_i, $1 \le i \le n$".

We can prove the following.

Lemma 6.8 *Let s be a state in A_G, and let w be a nonempty sequence of transitions from s in A_G. For all $w_i \in [w]_s$ from s in A_G, let t_i denote the first transition of w_i. Let Persistent_Set(s) be a nonempty persistent set in s. If none of the t_i are in Persistent_Set(s), then all transitions in Persistent_Set(s) are independent with all transitions in w.*

Proof:

The proof is by contradiction. Suppose there exist transitions in w that are dependent with some transitions in Persistent_Set(s) or that are in Persistent_Set(s). Let t_k

be the first such transition in w. Hence, all transitions before t_k in w are independent with all transitions in Persistent_Set(s), and are not in Persistent_Set(s).

If t_k is in Persistent_Set(s), then the sequence $w' = t_k t_1 \ldots t_{k-1} t_{k+1} \ldots t_n$, i.e., the sequence w where the transition t_k has been moved to the first position, is in $[w]_s$, and t_k is the first transition of a $w_i \in [w]_s$. This contradicts the assumption that none of the t_i is in Persistent_Set(s).

If t_k is not in Persistent_Set(s), since t_k is dependent in s_k with some transition t in Persistent_Set(s), the sequence of transitions $t_1 t_2 \ldots t_{k-1}$, which includes only transitions not in Persistent_Set(s) and which leads from s to s_k in A_G, is in contradiction with the fact that Persistent_Set(s) is a persistent set in s, by the definition of a persistent set (cf. Definition 4.1). ∎

Moreover, thanks to the "weakly uniform" assumption, we also have the following.

Lemma 6.9 *Let s be a state in A_G, and let w be a nonempty sequence of transitions from s in A_G. For all $w_i \in [w]_s$ from s in A_G defined from a valid conditional dependency relation that is weakly uniform, let t_i denote the first transition of w_i. Let Persistent_Set(s) be a nonempty persistent set in s. If none of the t_i are in Persistent_Set(s), then for all transitions t in Persistent_Set(s), we have $[w]_s \supseteq [w]_{s'}$ with $s \xrightarrow{t} s'$.*

Proof:

By Lemma 6.8, for all transitions t in Persistent_Set(s), t is independent with all transitions in w from s, and hence w is a sequence from s' in A_G, with $s \xrightarrow{t} s'$.

By definition, all $w' \in [w]_{s'}$ can be obtained from w by successively permuting pairs of *adjacent* independent transitions. It is thus sufficient to prove that, for any two words $w_1, w_2 \in [w]_{s'}$ that differ only by the order of *two* adjacent independent transitions, if $w_1 \in [w]_s$ then $w_2 \in [w]_s$.

Hence, let us assume that $w_1 = t_1 \ldots ab \ldots t_n$ and $w_2 = t_1 \ldots ba \ldots t_n$. We have from s' in A_G

$$s' \xrightarrow{t_1} s_1 \xrightarrow{t_2} s_2 \ldots \xrightarrow{t_j} s_j \xrightarrow{a} s_{j+1} \xrightarrow{b} s_{j+2} \ldots \xrightarrow{t_n} s_n$$

and

$$s' \xrightarrow{t_1} s_1 \xrightarrow{t_2} s_2 \ldots \xrightarrow{t_j} s_j \xrightarrow{b} s'_{j+1} \xrightarrow{a} s_{j+2} \ldots \xrightarrow{t_n} s_n.$$

Consider the states s'', s''' and s'''' in A_G such that $s \xRightarrow{t_1 \ldots t_j} s'' \xrightarrow{a} s''' \xrightarrow{b} s''''$. Since t is in Persistent_Set(s) and since none of the first transitions t_i of a $w_i \in [w]_s$ are in Persistent_Set(s), by Lemma 6.8, t is independent with all transitions in w. This implies that t and a are independent in s'', and that t and b are independent in s'''. Moreover, we have $s'' \xrightarrow{t} s_j$. Since t is independent with a in s'' and independent with b in s''', and that a and b are independent in s_j, a and b are independent in s'' since the valid dependency relation considered is weakly uniform. Consequently, $w_2 \in [w_1]_s = [w]_s$. ∎

Intuitively, the weakly uniform assumption is thus used to ensure that the number of interleavings of a trace $[w]_s$ does not increase after the execution of a transition that is independent with all the transitions in w. This property of (conditional) traces is then in turn used to prove the following lemma.

Lemma 6.10 *Let s be a state that is visited during the search performed by the algorithm of Figure 6.2. When s is backtracked, let $H(s).Sleep$ denote the sleep set stored with s in H, and let A_R denote the reduced state space that has been explored so far. Let w be a nonempty sequence of transitions from s in A_G. For all $w_i \in [w]_s$ from s in A_G, let t_i denote the first transition of w_i. If none of the t_i are in $H(s).Sleep$, then there exists a state s' in A_R such that the following conditions hold:*

1. *$s \xRightarrow{w'} s' \xrightarrow{t_1} s''$ in A_R where t_1 is one of the transitions t_i, and w' does not contain any transitions in w,*

2. *$[ww']_s = [w'w]_s$ from s in A_G, and*

3. *if we note $w_1 = t_1 w_1' \in [w]_{s'}$, and for all $w_i' \in [w_1']_{s''}$, t_i' denotes the first transition of w_i', none of the t_i' are in $s''.Sleep$, where $s''.Sleep$ denotes the sleep set associated with s'' after the execution of t_1 from s'.*

Proof:

The proof is by induction on the order in which states are backtracked.

Let s_1 be the first state that is backtracked during the search. When s_1 is backtracked, s_1 has been visited exactly once. Let $s_1.Sleep$ be the sleep set that was associated to s_1 when s_1 was visited. The value of $s_1.Sleep$ was saved with s_1 in H, and thus we have $H(s_1).Sleep = s_1.Sleep$. During this visit of s_1, a call to the function Persistent_Set_Satisfying_Proviso was performed. Let Persistent_Set_Satisfying_Proviso(s_1) denote the persistent set in s_1 satisfying the proviso that was returned. If there exists a transition t in Persistent_Set_Satisfying_Proviso(s_1) such that $t \notin s_1.Sleep$ and $s_1 \xrightarrow{t} s'$ and $s' \notin Stack$, such a transition t would have been executed from s_1, and

s' would have been backtracked before s_1, which is impossible. Therefore, because of the proviso, we know that all enabled transitions not in $s_1.Sleep$ have been executed from s_1 (they all lead to states in the *Stack*). Among these, let t_1 be the first transition t_i that has been executed from s_1 (we know that all transitions t_i have been executed from s_1 since $\forall t_i : t_i \notin s_1.Sleep$). Let s'' be the state reached after executing t_1 from s_1: $s_1 \xrightarrow{t_1} s''$. We have $w_1 = t_1 w'_1$. Let $s''.Sleep$ be the sleep set associated with s'' after the execution of t_1 from s_1. Let us show that, for all $w'_i \in [w'_1]_{s''}$, the first transition t'_i of w'_i is not in $s''.Sleep$.

Indeed, assume the opposite, i.e., there exists some transition $t'_i \in s''.Sleep$ such that t'_i is the first transition of a $w'_i \in [w'_1]_{s''}$. This implies that t'_i and t_1 are independent in s_1, else t'_i would not have been passed on to the sleep set associated to s''. Since they are independent in s_1, t'_i is enabled in s_1 and is the first transition of a path w_i. Given that t'_i is in $s''.Sleep$, either t'_i was in $s_1.Sleep$ or was added after being executed from s_1. The first possibility is in contradiction with the fact that t'_i is also the first transition of some $w_i \in [w]_{s_1}$ and thus is assumed not to be in $s_1.Sleep$. The second possibility is incompatible with the fact that t_1, not t'_i, is the first transition among the t_i to be executed from s_1.

Therefore, the lemma holds for the first backtracked state s_1 with $w' = \epsilon$. Now, let us prove that, if the lemma holds for the $(n-1)$st backtracked states, then it holds for the nth backtracked state s_n. Two cases are possible: either s_n has never been backtracked before, or it has already been backtracked during the search. We consider these two cases successively.

If s_n is backtracked for the first time, s_n has been visited exactly once. Let $s_n.Sleep$ be the sleep set that was associated to s_n when s_n was visited. The value of $s_n.Sleep$ was saved with s_n in H, and thus we have $H(s_n).Sleep = s_n.Sleep$. During this (first) visit of s_n, a call to the function Persistent_Set_Satisfying_Proviso was performed. Let Persistent_Set_Satisfying_Proviso(s_n) denote the persistent set in s_n satisfying the proviso that was returned. If at least one transition t_i is in Persistent_Set_Satisfying_Proviso(s_n), t_i has been explored from s_n since we know $t_i \notin s_n.Sleep$. By considering the first t_i which has been explored from s_n during this visit, and by applying a reasoning identical to the one done above for s_1, one concludes that the lemma holds for s_n. Consider the case where $\forall t_i : t_i \notin$ Persistent_Set_Satisfying_Proviso(s_n). This means that there exists at least one transition enabled in s_n and not in $s_n.Sleep$ that has not been explored from s_n. Hence, because of the proviso, there exists a transition $t \in$ Persistent_Set_Satisfying_Proviso(s_n) such that $t \notin s_n.Sleep$, $s_n \xrightarrow{t} s$ and $s \notin Stack$. Since $\forall t_i : t_i \notin$ Persistent_Set_Satisfying_Pro-

$viso(s_n)$, by lemma 6.8, t is independent with all transitions in w. Therefore, w is a sequence of transitions from s in A_G. Moreover, by Lemma 6.9, we know that $[w]_{s_n} \supseteq [w]_s$. Since none of the first transitions of sequences in $[w]_{s_n}$ are in $s_n.Sleep$ and since none of them are executed from s_n, none of the first transitions of sequences in $[w]_s$ are in the sleep set $s.Sleep$ that is associated with s after the execution of t from s_n. Since $s \notin Stack$, when s_n is backtracked, s has already been visited with the sleep set $s.Sleep$, and has already been backtracked. Consequently, none of the first transitions of sequences in $[w]_s$ are in $H(s).Sleep$ (since $H(s).Sleep \subseteq s.Sleep$). By applying the inductive hypothesis to state s with w as sequence of transitions in A_G, we know there exists a state s' in A_R such that $s \overset{w'}{\Rightarrow} s'$ and $s' \overset{t_1}{\rightarrow} s''$ in A_R where t_1 denotes one of the transitions t_i, $[ww']_s = [w'w]_s$ from s in A_G, and if we note $w_1 = t_1 w_1'$, for all the first transitions t_i' of a $w_i' \in [w_1']_{s''}$, $t_i' \notin s''.Sleep$, where $s''.Sleep$ denotes the sleep set associated with s'' after the execution of t_1 from s'. Since t is independent with all transitions in w, we have $[tw'w]_{s_n} = [tww']_{s_n} = [wtw']_{s_n}$. Consequently, the lemma holds in s_n.

Finally, consider the case where s_n has already been backtracked during the search. Let $H_{old}(s_n).Sleep$ be the sleep set stored with s_n in H the previous time s_n was backtracked. We know that $H(s_n).Sleep \subseteq H_{old}(s_n).Sleep$ (the sleep set stored with a state can only shrink between successive visits of that state). If for all transitions $t_i, t_i \notin H_{old}(s_n).Sleep$, the inductive hypothesis can be applied to state s_n already backtracked with $H_{old}(s_n).Sleep$ as sleep set stored with it in H, which directly proves the lemma for state s_n with $H(s_n).Sleep$. Else, there exists a transition t_i such that $t_i \in H_{old}(s_n).Sleep$. Since $t_i \notin H(s_n).Sleep$, t_i has been removed from $H_{old}(s_n).Sleep$, and has been executed from s_n during the last visit of s_n. If there are several such transitions t_i, consider the first one t_1 which has been executed at this last visit. Let s'' be the state reached after executing t_1 from s_n. The sleep set $s''.Sleep$ associated with s'' after the execution of t_1 from s_n is computed from the sleep set $H(s_n).Sleep$, which does not contain any transitions t_i. Therefore, by applying the same reasoning as the one done above for s_1, one concludes that the lemma holds for s_n with $H(s_n).Sleep$. ∎

The previous result is an important step towards a complete proof that reduced state spaces A_R explored by the algorithm of Figure 6.2 are trace automata. Indeed, we can now establish the following.

Theorem 6.11 *Let s be a state in the reduced state space A_R explored by the algorithm of Figure 6.2. Let $H(s).Sleep$ denote the sleep set stored with s in H once the search is completed. Let w be a sequence of transitions from s in A_G. For all $w_i \in [w]_s$ from s in A_G, let t_i denote the first transition of w_i. If none of the t_i are in $H(s).Sleep$, then there exists a sequence w' of transitions from s in A_R such that $w \in Pref([w']_s)$.*

Proof:

The proof proceeds by induction on the length of w. For $|w| = 0$, the result is immediate. Now, assume the theorem holds for paths (sequences of transitions) of length $n \geq 0$ and let us prove that it holds for a path w of length $n + 1$. For all $w_i \in [w]_s$ from s in A_G, let t_i denote the first transition of w_i.

Once the search is completed, all states in A_R have been backtracked. By applying lemma 6.10 to state s, we know that there exists a state s' in A_R such that $s \overset{w'}{\Rightarrow} s' \overset{t_1}{\rightarrow} s''$ in A_R where t_1 denotes one of the transitions t_i, $[ww']_s = [w'w]_s$ from s in A_G, and if we note $w_1 = t_1 w'_1$, for all the first transitions t'_i of a $w'_i \in [w'_1]_{s''}$, $t'_i \notin H(s'').Sleep$. This implies that w is a sequence in A_G from all intermediate states reached by w' from s, including s'. From the successor state s'' of s' by t_1, there is a sequence w'_1 in A_G such that $w_1 = t_1 w'_1 \in [w]_{s'}$. Since $|w'_1| = n$, and since $\forall t'_i : t'_i \notin H(s'').Sleep$, by applying the inductive hypothesis to state s'', we know there exists a sequence w'' explored from s'' in A_R such that $w'_1 \in Pref([w'']_{s''})$. In other words, there exists a sequence w''' from s'' in A_G such that $w''' \in [w'']''_s$ and $w''' = w'_1 w_{suff}$. From state s, we know that the sequence $w' t_1 w''$ is explored in A_R. From s, we have in A_G: $[w' t_1 w'']_s = [w' t_1 w''']_s = [w' t_1 w'_1 w_{suff}]_s = [w' w w_{suff}]_s$ (since $[w]_{s'} = [t_1 w'_1]_{s'}$) $= [ww'w_{suff}]_s$ (since $[w'w]_s = [ww']_s$). Obviously, $w \in Pref([ww'w_{suff}]_s)$, and thus $w \in Pref([w' t_1 w'']_s)$, $w' t_1 w''$ being explored in A_R from s. ∎

We can now easily conclude with the following thorem.

Theorem 6.12 *Let A_G be the global state space of a given system, and let A_R be the reduced state space explored by the algorithm of Figure 6.2 for this system. Then, A_R is a trace automaton for the system considered.*

Proof:

By applying Theorem 6.11 in the initial state s_0 of A_R and by Definition 6.4, one directly obtains that A_R is a trace automaton, since $H(s_0).Sleep = \emptyset$. ∎

6.4   Properties of Trace Automata

Many interesting properties of a concurrent system can be checked on a trace automaton for this system.

Theorem 6.13 *Let A_G be the global state space of a system, and let A_R be a trace automaton for this system. For all $t \in T$, t is executed in A_G iff t is executed in A_R.*

Proof:

Let t be a transition that occurs in A_G. Therefore, there exists a sequence w of transitions from s_0 in A_G that leads to a state s in A_G such that $s \xrightarrow{t} s'$. By definition of a trace automaton, there exists a sequence w' of transitions from s_0 in A_R such that w' is a linearization of a trace defined by an extension of wt. Consequently, t occurs in w', and thus in A_R.

The other direction of the theorem is immediate to establish since all sequences of transitions in A_R are sequences of transitions in A_G. ∎

The following theorem states that the reachability of local states can also be checked on a trace automaton.

Theorem 6.14 *Let A_G be the global state space of a system, and let A_R be a trace automaton for this system. For all processes P_i, for all local states $l \in P_i$, l is reachable from the initial state s_0 in A_G iff l is reachable from s_0 in A_R.*

Proof:

By definition, a local state $l \in P_i$ is reachable from the initial state s_0 in A_G iff there exists a global state s that is reachable from s_0 in A_G, and such that $s(i) = l$. Since l is reachable from s_0 in A_G, let w be the shortest sequence of transitions from s_0 to a state s in A_G such that $s(i) = l$. We have

$$s_0 \xrightarrow{t_1} s_1 \xrightarrow{t_2} s_2 \ldots \xrightarrow{t_{n-1}} s_{n-1} \xrightarrow{t_n} s.$$

We know that $s_{n-1}(i) \neq l$, else w would not be the shortest path leading from s_0 to l. Therefore, process P_i is active for transition t_n, and $l \in post(t_n)$. By Theorem 6.13, we know that there exists a state s' in A_R from which the transition t_n is executed in A_R. After executing t_n from s', a state s'' such that $s''(i) = l$ is reached in A_R.

The other direction of the theorem is immediate to establish since all states in A_R are states in A_G. ∎

Therefore, transitions that are never executed (dead code) can be checked for on a trace automaton. Moreover, checking if a given condition c, often called an *assertion*, is true in a particular local state l of a process P_i can be done by adding a new local state l_{error} to P_i and a new transition $(l, Not(c), skip, l_{error})$ to the system. Then, exploring a trace automaton for the modified system is sufficient to prove that such assertions are never violated. Many properties can be expressed by using assertions, like for instance, buffer overruns (i.e., attempts to send a message to a full queue), unspecified receptions, etc. Of course, adding transitions to a system introduces dependencies between these added transitions and other transitions, and has to be done as carefully as possible.

Global properties, i.e., properties that involve more than one process, can be checked by making them local as follows. If a property is not local to a process, one introduces an additional process in the system to which it is local. For instance, checking an invariant, i.e., if a given condition inv remains true in all states of A_G, can be done by adding a process $P_i = \{l, l_{error}\}$ with a single transition $(l, Not(inv), skip, l_{error})$ testing the truth value of the condition inv.

More generally, the verification of safety properties can be reduced to checking the reachability of a local state as follows [GW91b]. Safety properties can be represented by prefix closed automata on finite words [AS87]. We assume such a representation A_S and proceed as follows:

1. Build the automaton $A_{\neg S}$ corresponding to the complement of A_S. Since A_S is prefix closed, $A_{\neg S}$ is an automaton with only one accepting state (denoted X).

2. Check if the local state X is reachable in the new concurrent system composed of the original system and of the automaton $A_{\neg S}$.

Therefore, the verification of any safety property can be performed using a trace automaton A_R. Note that this framework is still applicable for safety properties represented by more than one automaton $A_{\neg S}$.

6.5 Comparison with Other Work

In [Val91], another "proviso" is given to be used with the (strong) stubborn set technique in order to check for properties more elaborate than deadlocks. More generally, this proviso can actually be used with all the algorithms computing persistent sets presented in Chapter 4, not only with the stubborn set algorithm of Section 4.5.

This proviso requires the detection of terminal maximal strongly connected components (TMSCC) in the explored reduced state space A_R, viewed as a directed graph.

A part G of A_R is a strongly connected component in A_R if all states in G are reachable from all states in G. A strongly connected component in A_R is said to be maximal if it is not properly included in any other strongly connected component. A strongly connected component G is said to be terminal if there is no outgoing transition from it, i.e., if there is no state not in G that is reachable from a state in G. Checking maximal strongly connected components in a directed graph can be done by using the well-known algorithm of Tarjan [Tar72, AHU74]. This algorithm is based on a depth-first search in the graph. Its time complexity is linear in the size of the reduced state space A_R. It requires the use of an additional stack and the storage of the value of a variable "DFNUMBER", which labels the reachable states in the order they are visited, with each state stored in randomly accessed memory. (See, e.g., [AHU74] for a complete presentation of this algorithm.)

The proviso of [Val91] consists in the following modification of the classical persistent-set selective search *not using sleep sets*, as shown in Figure 4.1 and performed in a depth-first order. In the following definition, the "root" of a TMSCC denotes the last state in the TMSCC that is backtracked during the depth-first selective search.

Definition 6.15 Each time a state s is backtracked during the search performed by the algorithm of Figure 4.1, if s is the root of a terminal maximal strongly connected component $TMSCC$ in A_R, and if there are transitions t that are enabled in s and never executed from any state in $TMSCC$, then another persistent set in s that contains at least one of such transitions t is computed, and the search continues from s to explore the transitions of this new persistent set that have not already been explored from s. ∎

Since the union of two persistent sets in s is a persistent set in s (it is easy to see this from the definition of persistent sets), this proviso is also equivalent to a restriction on the persistent sets that can be returned by the function Persistent_Set in a persistent-set selective search. Indeed, everything happens as if the value of Persistent_Set(s) was computed by successive approximations during the exploration of A_R (the value of Persistent_Set(s) is augmented if s is currently the root of a TMSCC).

It can be proved that the following theorem holds in all states in the reduced state space A_R explored by a persistent-set selective search using the above proviso (similar to Theorem 2.29 of [Val91]).

Theorem 6.16 *Let A_G be the global state space of a system, and let A_R be the reduced state space explored by a persistent-set selective search, as shown in Figure 4.1, using the proviso of Definition 6.15. Let s be a state in A_R. For all sequences w of transitions from s in A_G, there exists a sequence w' of transitions from s in A_R such that $w \in Pref([w']_s)$.*

Obviously, reduced state spaces A_R that satisfy the above theorem are trace automata. But the converse is not true, since the above theorem holds in *all states* in A_R, while the definition of trace automata requires that it holds *only in the initial state* s_0 of A_R. Therefore, the above theorem is stronger than is necessary for proving all the properties considered in the previous Section. The notion of trace automaton is weaker while sufficient for checking these properties, and thus allows more reduction in A_R.

Note that the proviso of Definition 6.2 can also be used without sleep sets, i.e., in conjunction with a persistent-set selective search, as shown in Figure 4.1. In this case, the first condition of the proviso of Definition 6.2 merely becomes that the set Persistent_Set(s) returned by the function Persistent_Set has to contain at least one transition not leading to the current *Stack*, and the "weakly uniform" assumption on the dependency relation used is no longer necessary. Indeed, by considering again the proofs given in Section 6.3 in the case where all sleep sets are always empty, one directly obtains a proof that the reduced state spaces A_R explored by a persistent-set selective search using this modified proviso are trace automata, and, moreover, that they satisfy Theorem 6.16.

In the case where sleep sets are not used, which one of these two provisos is then the "best"? If the explored reduced state space A_R does not contain any terminal maximal strongly connected components $TMSCC$ such that there are transitions t that are enabled in a state in $TMSCC$ and never executed from any state in $TMSCC$, then the proviso of Definition 6.15 will not force the selection of any additional transition, and its impact on A_R will be void; on the other hand, the proviso of Definition 6.2 modified as described above might force the selection of additional transitions if A_R contains cycles. If during the search there are terminal maximal strongly connected components $TMSCC$ such that there are transitions t that are enabled in a state in $TMSCC$ and never executed from any state in $TMSCC$, both provisos will force the selection of additional transitions and will have an impact on A_R. In this case, it is impossible to predict which proviso will yield the smaller A_R. Indeed, intuitively, the additional transitions forced by the proviso of Definition 6.2 will be executed from the first backtracked state of the $TMSCC$, while the additional transitions forced by the proviso of Definition 6.15 will be executed from the root of the $TMSCC$, i.e., the last backtracked state of the $TMSCC$. Hence, the two A_R that are obtained will then not be comparable in general (in the sense that one of them is not included in the other). Consequently, there is no "best" proviso: overall, it is impossible to predict which proviso will explore the smaller reduced state space.

Note that the proviso of Definition 6.2 is much simpler to implement than the proviso of Definition 6.15. Moreover, it does not require the use of any additional data structure. Finally, note that the proviso of Definition 6.15 is *not* compatible with sleep sets.

In [GW91b, GW93], the reachability of a local state l of a process P_i (and hence the verification of any safety property) is reduced to the deadlock detection problem by a transformation of the system description. This transformation consists of adding transitions in the original system (see [GW91b]). The new dependencies introduced in the system by these additional transitions ensure that if the local state l one is interested in is reachable from the initial state s_0, it will be visited during a selective search, without the need of any proviso.

It is not known whether the method of [GW91b] gives better reductions than the use of the proviso of Definition 6.2. An advantage of using a proviso during a selective search, and thus of generating a trace automaton, is that many properties (assertion violations, dead code, deadlocks, etc.) can be checked simultaneously during the same selective search. On the other hand, the transformation of the system described in [GW91b] depends on the local state l to be checked: the transitions that are added to the system during this transformation are there to prevent the selective search from missing l, if it is reachable, but are not sufficient for checking any other local states than l. The method of [GW91b] is thus more goal-oriented.

Finally note that the proviso of Definition 6.2 is simpler to implement than the system transformation of [GW91b].

Chapter 7

Model Checking

7.1 Beyond Safety Properties

Safety properties cover most of the properties of concurrent reactive systems that are verified in practice. It is nevertheless worth studying how partial-order methods can be adapted for checking *liveness properties*. Intuitively, whereas a safety property stipulates that "bad things" do not happen, a liveness property stipulates that "good things" do eventually happen [Lam77]. For instance, a liveness property can specify that each process of a concurrent system must always be able to eventually progress from its current local state. Such a property cannot be checked by only considering the finite behaviors of the system, as is the case for a safety property. Indeed, only *infinite* behaviors of the system can violate the above property.

Representing liveness properties and checking infinite behaviors of concurrent systems require the use of concepts and algorithms that are more complex than those for verifying safety properties. In this chapter, we discuss various techniques [Val90, GW91a, Pel93, Val93, Pel94, GW94] that have been proposed for the verification of liveness properties in the context of partial-order methods. Specifically, these techniques address the *model-checking problem* for *linear-time propositional temporal logic* [MP92]. Linear-time temporal-logic formulas can be used for specifying properties of infinite behaviors of a system, including arbitrary liveness properties. Given a concurrent system and a linear-time temporal-logic formula f, checking that all infinite computations of the system satisfy f is referred to as the model-checking problem.

The techniques presented in [Val90, GW91a, Pel93, Val93, Pel94, GW94] differ by the assumptions they make about the representation of the property to be checked, and by the verification strategies they adopt. In this chapter, we briefly present these techniques, and relate them with each other. We point out the key problems underlying the verification of liveness properties using partial-order methods, and compare the solutions that have been proposed for solving these problems. We also show how the proposed techniques complement each other.

7.2   Automata and Model Checking

To solve the model-checking problem, the only fact we need about linear-time temporal logic is that, for each formula f, it is possible to build a *Büchi automaton A_f* that accepts exactly the infinite words satisfying the temporal formula f [WVS83]. Formally, a Büchi automaton[Büc62] is a tuple $A = (\Sigma, S, \Delta, s_0, F)$, where

- Σ is an alphabet,

- S is a set of states,

- $\Delta \subseteq S \times \Sigma \times S$ is a transition relation,

- $s_0 \in S$ is the initial state, and

- $F \subseteq S$ is a set of accepting states.

A Büchi automaton is thus an automaton as defined in Section 2.2 augmented with a set F of accepting states. Büchi automata are used to define languages of ω-words, i.e., functions from the ordinal ω to the alphabet Σ. Intuitively, a word is *accepted* by a Büchi automaton if the automaton has an infinite execution that intersects set F infinitely often. Formally, we define a *computation σ* of A over an ω-word $w = a_1 a_2 \ldots$ as an ω-sequence $\sigma = s_0, s_1, \ldots$ (i.e., a function from ω to S) where $(s_{i-1}, a_i, s_i) \in \Delta$, for all $i \geq 1$. A computation $\sigma = s_0, s_1, \ldots$ is *accepting* if there is some state in F that repeats infinitely often, i.e., for some state $x \in F$ there are infinitely many $i \in \omega$ such that $s_i = x$. The ω-word w is *accepted* by A if there is an accepting computation of A over w.

A construction of a Büchi automaton A_f from a formula f can be found in [Wol89] and in Chapter 4 of [Tha89]. This construction is exponential in the length of the formula, but this is usually not a problem since the formulas to be checked are quite short and since the algorithm often behaves much better than its upper bound.

The verification procedure can then be the following [WVS83, VW86]. (This procedure is often referred to as the *automata-theoretic approach* to model checking.)

1. We first build a Büchi automaton for the *negation* of the formula f. The resulting automaton $A_{\neg f} = (\Sigma_{\neg f}, S_{\neg f}, \Delta_{\neg f}, s_{0\neg f}, F_{\neg f})$ accepts all sequences of states that violate f.

2. Then we compute the product automaton A_G of the original system and of the automaton $A_{\neg f}$ in such a way that the product automaton accepts all infinite computations of the system that are accepted by the automaton $A_{\neg f}$, i.e., all computations of the system that violate the formula f.

3. Finally, we check if the automaton A_G is empty, i.e., if it does not accept any sequence. If A_G is empty, we have proven that all infinite computations of P satisfy the formula f.

Of course, if the negation of the property $A_{\neg f}$ is directly provided by the user, the first step of the above procedure can be skipped.

Checking if the Büchi automaton A_G is nonempty amounts to checking if there exists a cycle in A_G (viewed as a graph) that is reachable from the initial state s_0 and that contains an accepting state. Actually, it is not necessary to consider all possible cycles in A_G, it is sufficient to check if A_G contains at least one maximal (nontrivial) strongly connected component that is reachable from the initial state and that includes a state from the set F. Equivalently, a Büchi automaton is nonempty if it has some accepting state that is reachable from the initial state and reachable from itself. Several algorithms can be used for checking emptiness of Büchi automata (see [GH93] for an overview), which can be done in linear time with respect to the size of the Büchi automaton. Note that computing A_G and checking its emptiness can be done at the same time.

Different definitions are possible for the product automaton A_G. In [GW91a, Val93], it is assumed that the automaton $A_{\neg f}$ is an additional process that synchronizes with the other processes of the system on transitions that have the same label, i.e., the same "action". Precisely, if A_{Sys} denotes the global state space of the concurrent system being verified, the product automaton A_G of the system $A_{Sys} = (\Sigma_{Sys}, S_{Sys}, \Delta_{Sys}, s_{0Sys})$ and of the new process $A_{\neg f} = (\Sigma_{\neg f}, S_{\neg f}, \Delta_{\neg f}, s_{0\neg f}, F_{\neg f})$ is the Büchi automaton $A_G = (\Sigma, S, \Delta, s_0, F)$ defined by

- $\Sigma = \Sigma_{Sys} \cup \Sigma_{\neg f}$,

- $S = S_{Sys} \times S_{\neg f}$,

- $((s, t), a, (u, v)) \in \Delta$ when

$\quad$ – $a \in \Sigma_{Sys} \cap \Sigma_{\neg f}$ and $(s, a, u) \in \Delta_{Sys}$ and $(t, a, v) \in \Delta_{\neg f}$,

$\quad$ – $a \in \Sigma_{Sys} \setminus \Sigma_{\neg f}$ and $(s, a, u) \in \Delta_{Sys}$ and $v = t$,

$\quad$ – $a \in \Sigma_{\neg f} \setminus \Sigma_{Sys}$ and $u = s$ and $(t, a, v) \in \Delta_{\neg f}$,

- $s_0 = (s_{0Sys}, s_{0\neg f})$,
- $F = S_{Sys} \times F_{\neg f}$.

Actions that appear both in A_{Sys} and in $A_{\neg f}$ are synchronized, others are interleaved. Transitions of A_{Sys} that synchronize with $A_{\neg f}$ are said to be *visible*. In this framework, transitions of the system and of the property are *"synchronized on actions"*.

In contrast, it is assumed in [Val90, Pel93, Pel94] that the automaton $A_{\neg f}$ is a special automaton whose transitions test the values of the variables of the system whenever the system executes a transition. Precisely, if A_{Sys} denotes the global state space of the concurrent system being verified, the product automaton A_G of the system $A_{Sys} = (\Sigma_{Sys}, S_{Sys}, \Delta_{Sys}, s_{0Sys})$ and of the automaton $A_{\neg f} = (\Sigma_{\neg f}, S_{\neg f}, \Delta_{\neg f}, s_{0\neg f}, F_{\neg f})$ is the Büchi automaton $A_G = (\Sigma, S, \Delta, s_0, F)$ defined by

- $\Sigma = \Sigma_{\neg f}$,
- $S = S_{Sys} \times S_{\neg f}$,
- $((s, w), a, (u, v)) \in \Delta$ when $(s, t, u) \in \Delta_{Sys}, (w, a, v) \in \Delta_{\neg f}$ and a evaluates to true in state s of A_{Sys},
- $s_0 = (s_{0Sys}, s_{0\neg f})$,
- $F = S_{Sys} \times F_{\neg f}$.

Transitions of the system that can affect the truth value of any state predicate appearing in the formula are said to be *visible*. In this framework, transitions of the system and of the property are *"synchronized on states"*.

Note that the automata-theoretic approach to model checking has the advantages of "on-the-fly verification". By this, we mean that we build the automaton A_G for the combination of the system and the property without ever building the automaton A_{Sys} for the system. Maybe surprisingly, the product automaton can be smaller than the automaton for the system alone because the property acts as a constraint on the behavior of the system. This approach of model checking thus has a head start over other approaches that require the automaton A_{Sys} to be built. In the context of partial-order methods, we will see that another advantage of the automata-theoretic approach is that the structure of the automaton $A_{\neg f}$ and its current local state can be exploited by partial-order methods to guide the selective search, and thus to improve its efficiency. The combination of on-the-fly verification with partial-order methods first appeared in [GW91a], and was later adopted in [Val93, Pel94] (the techniques of [Val90, Pel93] did not follow this paradigm).

7.3 Using Partial Orders for Model Checking

In practice, the limits of all model-checking methods come from the often excessive size of the product A_G. In order to use partial-order methods for doing model checking, we would like to be able to proceed as follows.

1. Build a Büchi automaton for the negation of the formula f. The resulting automaton is $A_{\neg f}$.

2. Compute a *trace automaton* A_R corresponding to the concurrent executions of the processes of the system, and of the automaton $A_{\neg f}$.

3. Check if the automaton A_R is empty.

Note that the temporal property represented by $A_{\neg f}$ can be sensitive to the order of *independent* transitions of the system. In the framework where transitions of the system and of the property are synchronized on actions, the fact that the order of actions that appear in $A_{\neg f}$ cannot be ignored while exploring the reduced state space is handled by treating $A_{\neg f}$ as any other process of the concurrent system [GW91a].

In the framework where transitions of the system and of the property are synchronized on states, the problem can be solved by considering all visible transitions (i.e., all transitions that can affect the truth value of any state predicate appearing in the formula) as being dependent, and by restricting the class of properties that can be checked to stuttering-invariant properties [Val90]. Informally, stuttering-invariance means that the truth value of a formula on an infinite sequence of states does not change if states in the sequence are repeated a finite number of times [Lam83]. Prohibiting stuttering is important in this framework since, without this restriction, all transitions could potentially affect the truth value of the formula, and hence would have to be considered as dependent, which would annihilate any benefit coming from the use of partial-order methods. In linear-time temporal logic, a simple way to restrict the properties that can be expressed in the logic to stuttering-invariant properties is to disallow the use of the "next" temporal operator [Lam83].

Once the above requirements are satisfied, can a trace automaton A_R for the system replace the product A_G for model checking?

It was shown in [GW91a] that a trace automaton A_R can be used for checking that all infinite behaviors of the system that contain an *infinite number* of occurrences of visible transitions satisfy the given property. In this case, verifying liveness properties can thus be done on the same reduced state space as for verifying safety properties.

If one is also interested in considering the infinite behaviors of the system that contain only a *finite number* of occurrences of visible transitions, using a trace automaton is not sufficient. It is then necessary to preserve more states and transitions in the reduced state space explored by a selective search. Several provisos have been proposed for this purpose. These provisos thus also preserve in A_R the presence of at least one cycle of invisible transitions that passes through an accepting state, if there exists one in A_G.

The first such proviso that has been proposed [Val90] was intended to be used in conjunction with the stubborn set technique (cf. Section 4.5), but can actually be used with other persistent-set algorithms as well. This proviso requires that:

1. at each state s reached during the search, if there is an enabled invisible transition, at least one invisible transition is executed from s in A_R; and

2. every cycle in A_R contains at least one state s that satisfies the following condition: the transitions explored from s in A_R are the enabled transitions of a stubborn set containing all visible transitions.

Intuitively, the first requirement preserves in A_R cycles of invisible transitions, while the second requirement ensures that, when exploring these cycles, visible transitions are not "ignored". In [Val90], an algorithm is given to detect cycles in A_R that do not satisfy Requirement 2 above. When such a cycle is detected, this algorithm forces the selection of new transitions from one of the states in the cycle to make it satisfy Requirement 2.

Another solution to satisfy Requirement 2 is to systematically select at each visited state the enabled transitions in a stubborn set containing all visible transitions [Val93]. However, this radical solution is very restrictive since it always forces the selection of a very specific type of persistent set at each visited state. This prevents the selection of many other persistent sets, including smaller ones, which is strongly in contradiction with the heuristics presented in Chapter 4.

Yet another solution to ensure Requirement 2, presented in [Pel94], is to prevent the selective search from closing cycles except from states where all enabled transitions are executed. In other words, at each visited state, the selected persistent set either has to contain exclusively transitions not leading to the current *Stack*, or has to be the set of all enabled transitions. This proviso can thus be viewed as a more restrictive version of the proviso of Definition 6.2, which was used for verifying safety properties.

Due to the lack of experimental data, it is not known how the performances of these different provisos for ensuring Requirement 2 compare with each other in practice.

Note that, when model-checking is performed on-the-fly, it is possible to optimize the selective search by using information about the current local state of $A_{\neg f}$ and the next transitions that can be executed from it. In the framework where transitions of the system and of the property are synchronized on actions, it is shown in [Val93] that it is necessary to ensure the first requirement only when the current local state of $A_{\neg f}$ is accepting, while it is necessary to enforce a proviso for ensuring Requirement 2 only when the current local state of $A_{\neg f}$ is not accepting. In the framework where transitions of the system and of the property are synchronized on states, it is shown in [Pel94] how the transitions outgoing from the current local state of $A_{\neg f}$ can be used to limit the number of transitions that need be explored.

7.4 Model Checking with Fairness Assumptions

It is useful in verification to take into account specific assumptions about the context in which processes of a concurrent system are executed. For instance, if concurrent processes are executed on different processors, it is customary to assume that, if a process has a transition that remains enabled, it will eventually execute it. This assumption is often referred to as *weak fairness* [MP92]. Various notions of fairness have been studied [Fra86, MP92]. The main purpose of these notions is to exclude behaviors of the concurrent system that would not be allowed by the specific type of process scheduler that is assumed. The fairness assumptions then act as filters, removing certain classes of infinite behaviors that conflict with the assumptions made about the process scheduler.

Like liveness properties, fairness assumptions can be modeled by linear-time temporal-logic formulas [LP85], or by Büchi automata [ACW90]. If fairness assumptions are modeled by a formula f', the verification problem amounts to checking that all infinite behaviors of the system satisfy the formula $f' \supset f$ (where $\supset$ denotes logical implication), which can be done as described in the previous section. If fairness assumptions are modeled by Büchi automata A_{fair} that are synchronized with the processes of the system[1], the definition of the product automaton A_G of the system, of the automata A_{fair}, and of the automaton $A_{\neg f}$ slightly differ from those given in Section 7.2 (since there are now several Büchi automata in the product), but the verification problem can be reduced again to checking the emptiness of A_G [GW91a].

At first glance, the interaction of the modeling of fairness assumptions and of partial-order methods is problematic since fairness assumptions often concern all processes involved in the system and hence may introduce many dependencies, which can wipe out the benefit of using partial-order methods. A solution to avoid this problem is to represent fairness assumptions in a distributed way, by assigning progress conditions to each process individually [GW91a]. This is equivalent to model fairness assumptions by a set of Büchi automata such that each Büchi automaton synchronizes with at most one process in the system. Such a way, fairness assumptions do not introduce any additional dependency among the transitions of the concurrent system [GW91a].

Note that the product of two Büchi automata accepts the intersection of the languages accepted by these two automata, and hence its effect is equivalent to a logical conjunction in temporal logic. Consequently, the translation of the solution given above in the temporal logic world becomes that, if a formula f is a conjunction of sub-formulas f_i, transitions of the system that can affect sub-formula f_k need not be considered as being dependent with transitions that can affect sub-formula f_l, with $k \neq l$, although these transitions are all visible. This observation also appeared in [Pel93] where it is recommended that each temporal-logic formula to be checked should be rewritten in an equivalent form with as many as possible boolean operators at the outermost levels of the formula, in order to express it as a conjunction of sub-formulas, which can then be treated separately when adding dependencies among visible transitions of the concurrent system.

Once the above requirements are satisfied, can a trace automaton A_R for the system replace the product automaton A_G for model checking with fairness assumptions? The answer to this question is negative because infinite computations involving *more than one process* are not necessarily preserved in A_R [GW91a]. Indeed, it is quite possible that the automaton A_G accepts some *fair* behavior of the system whereas A_R does not accept any *fair* behavior. This might seem counter-intuitive because

---

[1]Another similar possibility is to directly specify acceptance sets for the processes in the system, thus to define the system as being a product of Büchi automata [ACW90].

one could expect that, if A_G accepts some word w, then by permuting independent transitions of w, one would obtain an accepting computation of A_R, which would then be nonempty. This is actually true for finite computations but not for infinite computations. Indeed, consider two processes that are totally independent. A trace automaton for these two processes can be one that allows any number of transitions of the first process *followed* by any number of transitions of the second process. This is fine for finite computations, but for infinite computations, one will be left with either an infinite computation of the first process or one of the second process, but not an infinite computation of *both* processes. One can summarize this by saying that A_R represents the infinite computations of all processes, but not the joint infinite computations of unsynchronized processes [GW91a].

Trace automata do not adequately represent the ω-computations of the components from which they are built because infinite computations cannot be concatenated. Actually, with the help of a little abstraction, infinite computations could very well be concatenated. One can simply think of computations whose length is an ordinal larger than ω. This idea has been investigated in [GW91a, GW94]. Precisely, automata operating on words of length $\omega \times n$, $n \in \omega$, were defined and studied. It was shown that, when they are viewed as $\omega \times n$-automata, trace automata can be used for model checking with fairness assumptions. However, it is necessary to use a new model-checking algorithm, that checks for sequences of strongly connected components in trace automata.

Instead of using trace automata and a new, more complicated, model-checking algorithm, another solution consists in using an additional proviso during state-space exploration that ensures that enough states and transitions are preserved in the reduced state space A_R to make possible the use of classical model-checking algorithms on A_R. This is the approach adopted in [Pel93, Pel94], where a proviso is given for model-checking with fairness assumptions. This proviso forces the traversal of "fair cycles" by preventing the selective search to close cycles except from states from which all enabled transitions are executed. This proviso increases the size of the reduced state space that is explored, but is easy to implement [HP94].

Chapter 8

Experiments

8.1 How Can Partial-Order Methods Be Evaluated?

How much can one gain by using the methods described in this work? It is very difficult to give a general answer. Indeed, one can quite easily construct families of systems for which nothing is gained whatsoever. Examples of such systems are systems where the coupling between the processes is so tight that two independent transitions are never simultaneously enabled. (The system is in fact purely sequential.) In this case, partial-order methods yield no reduction, and the selective search becomes equivalent to a classical exhaustive search.

On the other hand, it is also easy to construct systems for which the growth of the state space when the number of processes in the system increases is reduced from exponential to polynomial by a selective search. This is the case, for instance, for the dining-philosophers system of Section 2.3. The number of states in the global state space A_G and in the reduced state space A_R explored by a selective search using persistent sets and sleep sets (without proviso) are given in Figure 8.1 for various numbers of philosophers (logarithmic scale).

Going one step further, it is also easy to find examples of systems for which the global state space increases in size when the value of some parameter grows, while the reduced state space remains the same. For instance, consider the following "producer-consumer" example.

Example 8.1 Consider a system containing a process "producer" $P = \{p_0\}$ and a process "consumer" $C = \{c_0\}$, an object "bounded FIFO channel" of size $N = 1000$,

States

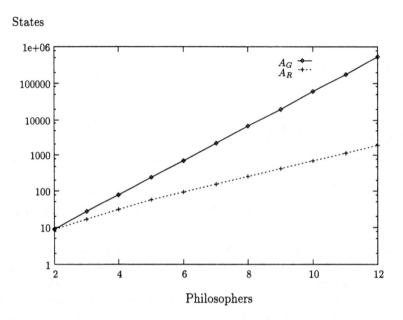

Figure 8.1: Reduction due to partial-order methods for dining philosophers

denoted q, as considered in Examples 3.20 and 4.29, and two transitions

$$t_1 = (p_0, Not(Full(q)), Send(q, m), p_0), \quad t_2 = (c_0, Not(Empty(q)), Receive(q), c_0),$$

where it is assumed that $Send(q, m)$ denotes a command that performs a $Send$ operation on the object q with m as input, $Receive(q)$ denotes a command that performs a $Receive$ operation on the object q (the output of the $Receive$ operation on q is discarded here), $Full(q)$ denotes a boolean condition equivalent to the value returned by the execution of a $Full$ operation on object q, and $Empty(q)$ denotes a boolean condition equivalent to the value returned by the execution of an $Empty$ operation on object q. Let $s_0 = (p_0, c_0, ()) \in P \times C \times V_q$ be the initial state of the producer-consumer system (q is initially empty). Let us investigate what the reduced state space A_R explored by a selective search using persistent sets could be. In state s_0, only transition t_1 is enabled. After executing this transition, state $s_1 = (p_0, c_0, (m))$ is reached. In state s_1, both transitions t_1 and t_2 are enabled. Moreover, the set $\{t_2\}$ is a persistent set in s_1. After executing t_2 from s_1, state s_0 is reached again, and the exploration of A_R stops. This reduced state space A_R is shown in Figure 8.2. Dotted

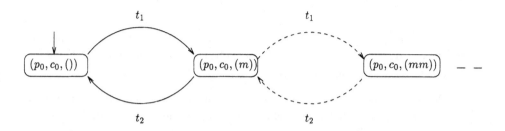

Figure 8.2: Reduced state space for the producer-consumer problem

transitions are not in A_R. Clearly, A_R is independent of the value of N, while the size of A_G is proportional to N. If $N = \infty$, i.e., if the channel (buffer) is unbounded, A_R is finite, while the global state space A_G is infinite. ∎

Clearly, by a biased choice of examples, an arbitrarily exaggerated impression of the improvements could thus be suggested. For instance, by setting the number of philosophers to a sufficiently large number, we can claim that we can check systems with astronomical numbers of states, like 10^{20} states as in [BCM+90]. With the producer-consumer example, we can even claim to be able to check systems with infinite numbers of states. Of course, this should be taken with a grain of salt since the fact that checking only a small part of such enormous state spaces is sufficient only indicates that most of the states in the global state space are uninteresting. This observation leads us to the following conclusion: the number of states in the global state space of a system does not give a good measure of its complexity.

Along the same line of thought, the study of the asymptotic behavior of the function giving the number of states for different numbers of processes in a system is only of limited practical interest. Indeed, state-space exploration techniques are rarely used to verify systems composed of tens of identical processes. For such systems, it is preferable to use other verification techniques specially tailored for proving properties of systems with undefined numbers of participants (e.g., [KM89, WL89]).

Consequently, experiments with realistic examples, including industrial-size ones, appear to be the most informative approach to evaluating partial-order verification methods.

8.2   A Partial-Order Package for SPIN

In order to perform experiments on complex concurrent systems, we have implemented (most of) the algorithms presented in the previous chapters in an add-on package for the protocol verification system SPIN.

SPIN is an automated verification system for communication protocols described in the Promela language [Hol91]. Promela is a full nondeterministic guarded-command language. Promela defines systems of asynchronously executing concurrent processes that can interact via shared variables and message channels. Interaction via message channels can be either synchronous (i.e., by rendez-vous) or asynchronous (buffered) with arbitrary (user-specified) buffer capacities, and arbitrary numbers of message parameters. These different types of communication can be combined. Given a concurrent system described by a Promela program, SPIN can verify properties of the system by performing a classical depth-first search in the global state space of the system. By default, SPIN checks for deadlocks, dead code, and violations of user-specified assertions (cf. Chapter 6).

The partial-order package we have developed for SPIN checks by default the same properties as SPIN does, i.e., it checks for deadlocks, dead code, and violations of user-specified assertions. These properties are checked by exploring only a trace automaton for the system being analyzed, instead of its global state space. The partial-order package includes the implementation of a selective search using persistent sets, sleep sets, and the proviso of Definition 6.2, as shown in Figure 6.2. For computing persistent sets, an algorithm similar to Algorithm 2 using the $\rhd_s$ relation presented in Chapter 4 has been chosen to be implemented. Indeed, we showed in Chapter 4 that there is no "best" algorithm for computing persistent sets. For the class of examples we have considered, it turns out that Algorithm 2 provides a good trade-off between the complexity of the algorithm, its additional run-time expense, and the reduction it can yield (see next Section). The proviso of Definition 6.2 has been chosen to be implemented in the partial-order package because of its simplicity, its efficiency (see next Section), and its compatibility with sleep sets (and with the state-space caching technique considered in Section 8.4). (The verification of liveness properties is not supported by the current version of the package.)

A few minor changes to the Promela language have been made in order to make systems described in Promela compatible with the assumptions under which the algorithms of this work have been developed. For instance, process creation has been forbidden, and the use of the "atomic" Promela expression has been defined more

strictly. Promela has also been extended with two predicates *Empty* and *Full* on
FIFO channels, for which optimizations are implemented in the package (cf. Chapters 3 and 4).

Our partial-order package is available free of charge for educational and research
purposes by anonymous ftp from ftp.montefiore.ulg.ac.be in the /pub/po-package directory. More information on the partial-order package can be found in the README
file in this directory.

8.3 Evaluation

The partial-order package has been tested on various realistic examples of protocols[1].
The aim of these experiments was to determine the type of reduction that can be
expected on real protocol examples when using the algorithms presented in this work,
and to evaluate the respective impact of these algorithms on the reduction obtained.
In this Section, results obtained with four sample protocols are detailed.

- PFTP is a file transfer protocol presented in Chapter 14 of [Hol91], modeled in
  206 lines of Promela. It consists of three processes communicating via FIFO
  channels.

- MULOG3 is a model of a mutual exclusion algorithm presented in [TN87], for
  3 participants, modeled in 97 lines of Promela. It consists of six processes
  communicating via FIFO channels and shared variables.

- ABRA is a model of the Abracadabra protocol presented in [Tur93], modeled
  in 168 lines of Promela. It consists of four processes communicating via FIFO
  channels.

- DTP is a data transfer protocol, modeled in 406 lines of Promela. It consists of
  three processes communicating via FIFO channels.

Experiments were performed using six different algorithms.

- DFS denotes a classical search, as shown in Figure 2.1, performed in a depth-
  first order.

---

[1]We wish to thank Gerard Holzmann for providing us with several of these examples.

- SLEEP denotes a selective search using sleep sets alone, as considered in Theorem 5.4 (equivalent to the algorithm of Figure 5.2 when the function Persistent_Set returns the set of all enabled transitions).

- PS denotes a persistent-set selective search, as shown in Figure 4.1.

- PS+SLEEP denotes a selective search using persistent sets and sleep sets, as shown in Figure 5.2.

- PS+PROV denotes a selective search using persistent sets and the proviso of Definition 6.2.

- PS+SLEEP+PROV denotes a selective search using persistent sets, sleep sets and the proviso of Definition 6.2, as shown in Figure 6.2.

All these algorithms can be viewed as particular cases of the general selective-search algorithm using persistent sets, sleep sets and the proviso, i.e., PS+SLEEP+PROV. They can be obtained in our partial-order package by turning off the use of persistent sets, sleep sets, and/or the proviso. This is done by using appropriate options at compile-time (there is no run-time overhead due to turning off some partial-order methods). For instance, DFS corresponds to a selective-search where all partial-order methods are turned off. Note that DFS is, on average, two times slower than the original version of SPIN. This is due to the fact that parts of the original code of SPIN had to be modified and re-written in order to connect the partial-order selective-search algorithms to the rest of the tool. The new code has not been optimized.

Results of these experiments are presented in Table 8.1. All experiments were performed on a SPARC2 workstation with 64 Megabytes of RAM, using the Partial-Order Package version 3.0. For each run, the numbers of visited states and traversed transitions are given. Time (in seconds) is user time plus system time as reported by the UNIX-system time command. All visited states are stored in a hash table. To avoid significant run-time penalties for disk-access, visited states can only be stored in randomly accessed memory, i.e., in the main memory available in the computer on which the experiments are performed. Consequently, parameter settings in all the protocols considered were chosen to produce global state spaces that can easily be stored in 64 Megabytes of RAM. For each run, the amount of memory used is directly proportional to the number of stored states. Indeed, transitions are not stored in memory. Moreover, when using sleep sets, the amount of memory used for storing sleep sets is insignificant with respect to the overall memory requirements of the selective search, since a handful of bytes suffices to represent one sleep set for

Protocol	Algorithm	Stored States	Transitions	Time
PFTP	DFS	446,982	1,257,317	478.2
	SLEEP	446,982	622,364	639
	PS	276,722	482,722	662.7
	PS+SLEEP	249,994	351,633	684.7
	PS+PROV	279,808	490,228	673.8
	PS+SLEEP+PROV	250,514	352,371	690.1
MULOG3	DFS	38,181	111,668	25.3
	SLEEP	38,181	38,241	30.5
	PS	18,537	38,906	25.8
	PS+SLEEP	17,984	18,057	26
	PS+PROV	18,537	38,906	26
	PS+SLEEP+PROV	17,984	18,057	26.4
ABRA	DFS	149,816	372,010	494.2
	SLEEP	149,816	176,469	546
	PS	32,289	40,931	166.3
	PS+SLEEP	27,781	34,381	155.7
	PS+PROV	40,472	52,355	204.3
	PS+SLEEP+PROV	36,913	46,934	204.4
DTP	DFS	251,409	648,467	200.2
	SLEEP	251,409	269,912	189
	PS	9,904	10,351	11.3
	PS+SLEEP	9,904	10,351	11.5
	PS+PROV	9,904	10,351	11.4
	PS+SLEEP+PROV	9,904	10,351	11.7

Table 8.1: Evaluation

these examples (there are at most a handful of enabled transitions in each state), while more than one hundred bytes are used to represent one state (each state is composed of the current local state of all processes, all current variable values, and all current message-channel contents).

From the numbers given in Table 8.1, three main observations can be made concerning the respective impact of persistent sets, sleep sets, and the proviso of Definition 6.2 on the reduction obtained.

- *Persistent Sets yield the most important reductions on the number of visited states. They can also yield good reductions on the number of explored transitions.*

- *Sleep sets yield a less impressive reduction on the number of visited states, but yield very good reductions on the number of explored transitions.*

- *Using the proviso of Definition 6.2 usually does not yield an important increase of the number of visited states and transitions.*

The last observation shows that the proviso of Definition 6.2 is an efficient solution for verifying safety properties using partial-order methods.

As predicted by Theorem 5.4, SLEEP does not yield any reduction on the number of visited states with respect to DFS. For all protocols, the best reductions can be obtained with PS+SLEEP, i.e., by using simultaneously persistent sets and sleep sets. Using persistent sets and sleep sets gives better reductions than using persistent sets alone in almost all cases. For DTP, persistent sets are so good in reducing the number of states and transitions that sleep sets are not able to improve this result (cf. the discussion of Section 5.3.1).

These results show that using the partial-order methods developed in this work is basically a no-risk improvement. In the worst case, when the reduction is not sufficient to make up the additional run time overhead (PFTP), the selective search can be slightly slower than a classical search, but the overall time complexity remains linear in the number of explored transitions.

Moreover, using partial-order methods can strongly decrease *both* the time and the memory resources needed to verify properties of concurrent systems (DTP). Therefore, they can be used to verify more complex protocols.

8.4 State-Space Caching

Another observation that can be made from the results given in Table 8.1 is the following: when using partial-order methods, and especially when using sleep sets, the number of state matchings, i.e., the number of visited transitions minus the number of visited states, strongly decreases. This phenomenon was already pointed out in Section 5.3.2, and can be explained as follows.

When performing a classical search (like DFS), almost all states in the state space of a concurrent system are typically visited several times. There are two causes for this:

1. From the initial state, the explorations of all interleavings of a single finite concurrent execution of the system always lead to the same state. This state will thus be visited several times because of all these interleavings.

2. From the initial state, explorations of different finite concurrent executions may lead to the same state.

When using partial-order methods, and especially when using sleep sets, most of the effects of the first cause given above can be avoided, and, in many cases, most of the states are visited *only once* during the selective search.

States that are visited only once do not need to be stored in memory. Indeed, the only reason why visited states are stored in memory is to avoid redundant explorations of parts of the state space: when a state that has already been visited is visited again later during the search, it is not necessary to revisit all its successors. Unfortunately, it is impossible to determine which states are visited only once before the search is completed. However, if most of the states are visited only once, the probability that a state will be visited again later during the search is very small, and the risk of double work when not storing an already visited state becomes very small as well. This enables one not to store most of the states that have already been visited without incurring too much redundant explorations of parts of the state space. The memory requirements can thus strongly decrease without seriously increasing the time requirements.

State-space caching [Hol85, JJ91] is a memory management technique for storing the states encountered during a depth-first search that consists in storing all the states of the current explored path (i.e., those in the current depth-first search "stack") plus as many other states as possible given the remaining amount of available memory. It

Transitions

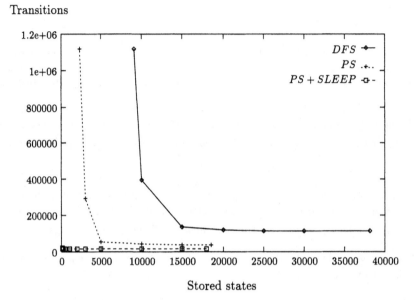

Stored states

Figure 8.3: Performances of state-space caching for MULOG3

thus creates a restricted *cache* of selected system states that have already been visited. Initially, all states encountered are stored into the cache. When the cache fills up, old states that are not in the stack are removed from the cache to accommodate new ones. This method never tries to store more states than possible in the cache. Thus, if the size of the cache is greater than the maximal size of the stack during the exploration, the search is not truncated, and eventually terminates.

We have implemented such a caching discipline in the partial-order package. The caching discipline can be used with any of the selective-search algorithms that were considered in the previous Section. Results of experiments with different cache sizes and the algorithms DFS, PS, and PS+SLEEP for the MULOG3 protocol are presented in Figure 8.3. For each run, the run time is directly proportional to the number of explored transitions.

With DFS, these results clearly show that the size of the cache, i.e., the number of stored states, can be reduced to approximately the third of the total number of states in A_G without seriously affecting the number of explored transitions and hence the run time. If the cache is further reduced, the run time increases dramatically, due to redundant explorations of large parts of the state space. This run-time explosion makes state-space caching inefficient under a certain threshold.

With PS, this threshold can be reduced to approximately the eighth of the total number of states. This improvement is not very spectacular because the number of matched states, even when using PS, is still too important (see Table 8.1). The risk of double work when reaching an already visited state that has been removed from the cache is not reduced enough.

With PS+SLEEP, the situation is different: there is no run-time explosion anymore. Indeed, the number of matched states is reduced so much (see Table 8.1) that the risk of double work becomes very small. When the cache size is reduced up to the maximal depth of the search (this maximal depth is the lower bound for the cache size since all states of the stack are stored to ensure the termination of the search), the increase of the number of explored transitions is still less than 10% with respect to the number of transitions explored by PS+SLEEP when all visited states are stored in memory, i.e., without using state-space caching.

In other words, the MULOG3 protocol, which has 38,181 reachable states that can be visited by DFS in 25 seconds (see Table 8.1), can be analyzed with the same run time by using PS+SLEEP and state-space caching while storing no more than 150 states. *The memory requirements are reduced by a factor of 200 while the run time remains the same.*

Of course, the practical interest of this result is that *using partial-order methods and state-space caching together makes possible the complete exploration of very large state spaces*, that could not be explored so far.

For instance, consider two other versions of the MULOG protocol, denoted MU-LOG4 and MULOG5, with respectively four and five participants. Let PS+SLEEP+-Caching denote a selective search using persistent sets, sleep sets, and state-space caching. Tables 8.2 and 8.3 present results of experiments performed on MULOG4 and MULOG5 with the algorithms DFS, PS+SLEEP, and PS+SLEEP+Caching. "Stored states" is the number of stored states at the end of the search. When state-space caching is used, the maximum number of stored states, i.e., the size of the cache, is limited to 300,000 states. (This number is approximately the maximum number of states that can be stored in RAM for MULOG4 and MULOG5 while still avoiding any paging.) "Cleared states" is the number of times a state was removed from the cache. "Matched states" is the number of state matchings that occurred during the search.

Algorithm	Stored St.	Cleared St.	Matched St.	Transitions	Time
DFS	–	–	–	–	–
PS+SLEEP	654,600	0	6,189	660,789	986.4 (2516.7)
PS+SLEEP+Caching	300,000	354,676	6,198	660,874	1122.6 (1184.4)

Table 8.2: Verification of MULOG4

Algorithm	Stored St.	Cleared St.	Matched St.	Transitions	Time
DFS	–	–	–	–	–
PS+SLEEP	–	–	–	–	–
PS+SLEEP+Caching	300,000	28,613,162	349,904	29,263,066	60,633.1

Table 8.3: Verification of MULOG5

For MULOG4, DFS was not able to complete its search, since its global state space is too large to be stored in (64 Megabytes of) memory. Using state-space caching with DFS does not help, because of the run time explosion mentioned above. MULOG4 can still be verified using PS+SLEEP, even without state-space caching. Real time as reported by the UNIX-system time command is given between parentheses below the run time (user time plus system time). The important difference between these two numbers for PS+SLEEP is due to paging (storing 654,600 states of MULOG4 requires more than 64 Megabytes of RAM, so some of them had to be stored on disk).

For MULOG5, the only algorithm that is able to completely verify the correctness of this protocol is PS+SLEEP+Caching. The complete selective search takes approximately 17 hours, and explores 29,263,066 transitions. This means that the *reduced* state space A_R explored by PS+SLEEP contains at most 29,263,066 states. The size of the global state space A_G of MULOG5 is not known, but is very likely several orders of magnitude larger than the largest state spaces that can be explored by other existing verification tools.

Note that the efficiency of the state-space caching technique can be dynamically estimated during the search: if the maximum stack size remains acceptable with respect to the cache size and if the proportion of matched states remains small enough, the run-time explosion will likely be avoided. Else one cannot predict if the cache size is large enough to avoid the run-time explosion.

8.5 Conclusion

Using partial-order methods is basically a no-risk improvement with respect to a classical exhaustive search in the state space of the system being analyzed. Moreover, partial-order methods can yield substantial improvements in the performances of the verification. Therefore, these methods broaden the applicability of state-space exploration techniques to more complex systems.

The reduction obtained depends on the coupling between the processes in the system. When the coupling is very tight, partial-order methods yield no reduction, and the selective search becomes equivalent to a classical exhaustive search. When the coupling between the processes is very loose, the reduction can be very impressive. For most realistic examples, partial-order methods provide a significant reduction of the memory and time requirements needed to verify protocols.

It is worth noticing that partial-order methods can already yield good performance improvements for verifying systems containing only a handful of processes. It is not necessary to consider systems composed of tens of processes to obtain spectacular reductions. To put it in another way, the part of the state explosion due to the exploration of all possible interleavings of independent transitions can already be very important for systems containing only a few processes, and partial-order methods are able to get rid of most of this explosion.

This very important point emphasizes the practical significance of partial-order methods. Indeed, most of the protocol models that are analyzed with state-space exploration techniques typically contain only a handful of processes. The examples we have considered in Section 8.3 reflect this reality. For instance, a typical protocol example, as illustrated in Figure 8.4, is usually composed of a few processes that communicate asynchronously by exchanging messages through some communication medium, each process being described by a long piece of sequential code, with complex interactions between control and data.

Not only these systems are very frequent, but they are also very hard to verify: they are complex (several hundreds lines of (Promela) code are needed to model these systems), and their state spaces are highly irregular. Specifically, their state spaces seem to be much more irregular than, for instance, those of systems composed of many identical processes (or pieces of hardware), for which symbolic verification

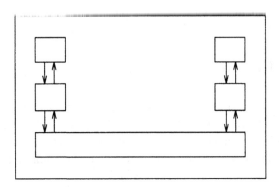

Figure 8.4: Typical protocol example

techniques are able to capture the regularity of the state space with the guidance of the user (see, e.g., [BCM+90]). In contrast, for examples of the type we are considering here, existing symbolic verification techniques turned out to be inferior to classical state-space exploration algorithms [HD93]. Consequently, for this particular, though important, class of systems, partial-order methods are one of the most successful approaches to tackle the state explosion arising during the analysis of such systems.

For other types of systems, it is not known how competitive partial-order methods are. For instance, it is claimed in [McM92] that partial-order methods like those presented in this work would not give good reductions for asynchronous circuit models, "because of the ubiquity of confusion in such models." This argument is not sufficient to justify such a claim. Indeed, it should be proved, for instance, that for all systems in a specific class of concurrent systems (left to be defined), for all states s in the global state spaces of these systems, the only nonempty persistent set in s is the set of all transitions enabled in s. Then, indeed, by Theorem 5.4, the algorithms considered in this work will visit all reachable states of such systems (though not necessarily all transitions in their state spaces), and yield no reduction in the number of visited states. However, without such a proof (a precise characterization of such a class of systems is not given in [McM92]), and without any experimental result validating this claim, the problem is still open.

Finally, we have shown in this chapter that using partial-order methods, and especially using sleep sets, can substantially improve the state-space caching discipline by getting rid of the main cause of its previous inefficiency, namely prohibitive state matching due to the exploration of all possible interleavings of concurrent executions all leading to the same state. Thanks to sleep sets, the memory requirements needed to verify large *reduced* state spaces can be strongly decreased (several orders of magnitude) without seriously affecting the time requirements. This makes possible the complete exploration of very large reduced state spaces (several tens of million states) in a reasonable time (one night). Used together, partial-order methods and state-space caching significantly push back the limits of verification by state-space exploration.

Chapter 9

Conclusions

9.1 Summary

We have built, from the ground up, an original approach to cope with the state-explosion problem that arises during the verification of concurrent systems by classical state-space exploration techniques. Specifically, our approach tackles one cause of the state-explosion problem: the modeling of concurrency by interleaving. Indeed, all interleavings of all concurrent transitions of a system are represented in its state space. We showed that exploring all these interleavings is not necessary for verification.

The focus of this work has been on developing practical and efficient selective-search algorithms for exploring only a reduced part of the state space of a concurrent system that is sufficient for checking given properties of this system. The algorithms we have presented rely on the concept of independency and the properties it implies. They take advantage of the independency between transitions to avoid exploring all their interleavings. The interleavings of a partial-order execution were related by the notion of Mazurkiewicz's trace. Traces proved to be a powerful and elegant vehicle to carry out the correctness proofs of our algorithms. Several ways to detect independency in concurrent systems were discussed and illustrated using a general model for representing concurrent systems.

Two compatible techniques for determining the transitions that need to be explored in a selective search were developed: persistent sets and sleep sets. Persistent sets were introduced to provide an abstract characterization of a whole family of existing algorithms. All these algorithms were shown to compute persistent sets, and were precisely compared with each other. Then it was shown how all the previous algorithms can be improved by using a new relation that models interactions between transitions more finely than the existing relations. The notion of conditional stubborn set was introduced, and all the considered algorithms were shown to be approximations of conditional stubborn sets.

The second main algorithmic technique developed in this work is the sleep set technique. We have described how to combine sleep sets with persistent sets, and have studied the properties of sleep sets. Results of experiments with real protocol examples show that not only persistent sets and sleep sets are compatible, but they are also complementary.

A simple modification of a selective-search algorithm that can be used for checking the reachability of local states, and, more generally, for checking safety properties, was presented. The modification consists in enforcing a simple additional proviso that ensures that the choices between enabled independent transitions made during the selective search are not completely unfair with respect to some processes. The notion of trace automaton was shown to characterize the joint effect of using persistent sets and sleep sets for the verification of safety properties.

The verification of liveness properties and, more generally, the model-checking problem for linear-time temporal-logic were then addressed. Techniques for solving these problems were discussed and compared. It was also shown how the proposed techniques complement each other.

The algorithms developed in this work have been implemented in an add-on package for the protocol verification system SPIN. This partial-order package has been tested on a large set of protocol examples, including the four sample examples detailed in the previous chapter. Results of experiments show that using the partial-order methods we have developed is basically a no-risk improvement with respect to a classical exhaustive search in the state space of the system being analyzed. Moreover, partial-order methods can yield substantial improvements in the performances of the verification. The improvement obtained depends on the coupling between the processes in the system. When the coupling is very tight, partial-order methods yield no reduction, and the selective search becomes equivalent to a classical exhaustive search. When the coupling between the processes is very loose, the reduction in the number of explored states and transitions can be very impressive. For most realistic examples, partial-order methods provide a significant reduction of the memory and time requirements needed to verify protocols.

Finally, we have shown that using partial-order methods, and especially using sleep sets, can substantially improve the state-space caching discipline by getting rid of the main cause of its previous inefficiency, namely prohibitive state matching due to the exploration of all possible interleavings of concurrent executions all leading to the same state. Used together, partial-order methods and state-space caching significantly broaden the applicability of verification by state-space exploration.

9.2 Future Work

This section indicates some directions for future research.

Tackling other causes of state explosion

In real protocols, the modeling of concurrency by interleaving is only but one cause of the state explosion that creeps in during verification by state-space exploration. Developing techniques to tackle the other causes of state explosion (e.g., variables whose values range over a large domain, communication channels that contain many different types of messages, etc.), and combining them with partial-order methods is certainly worthwhile. Simultaneously attacking the different causes of state-explosion should substantially improve the efficiency and the applicability of automatic verification tools.

Verifying other properties

So far, partial-order methods have been developed for deadlock detection, for the verification of safety properties, and for linear-time temporal-logic model checking. These three types of properties cover most of the properties of concurrent reactive systems one would ever wish to verify in practice. It is nevertheless interesting to study how partial-order methods can be adapted for checking other types of properties, like properties expressed in branching-time temporal logic or in partial-order temporal logic. A first step in this direction is presented in [GKPP94].

Another area for further research is the verification of "real-time" systems, i.e., systems whose descriptions involve a quantitative notion of time. Investigations in this direction have started recently with [YSSC93] where a verification technique for real-time systems using partial-order methods is presented.

Other applications

State explosion is a long-standing problem, which is central to many applications in computer science. Any method that can tackle this problem in a neat way is of great promise, not only for verification but also for several other applications. We believe partial-order methods may be useful for solving other problems than verification. Actually, any problem that can be reduced to a state-space exploration problem and where some form of independency (commutativity) can be identified is a potential target for partial-order methods. An example of such an application is planning [GK91]. Several other research topics of this nature are also possible.

Bibliography

[ACW90]   S. Aggarwal, C. Courcoubetis, and P. Wolper. Adding liveness properties to coupled finite-state machines. *ACM Transactions on Programming Languages and Systems*, 12(2):303–339, 1990.

[AFdR80] K. R. Apt, N. Francez, and W. P. de Roever. A proof system for communicating sequential processes. *ACM Transactions on Programming Languages and Systems*, 2:359–385, 1980.

[AHU74]   Alfred V. Aho, John E. Hopcroft, and Jeffrey D. Ullman. *The Design and Analysis of Computer Algorithms*. Addison-Wesley, 1974.

[AS87]   B. Alpern and F. B. Schneider. Recognizing safety and liveness. *Distributed Computing*, 2:117–126, 1987.

[BCM⁺90] J.R. Burch, E.M. Clarke, K.L. McMillan, D.L. Dill, and L.J. Hwang. Symbolic model checking: 10^{20} states and beyond. In *Proceedings of the 5th Symposium on Logic in Computer Science*, pages 428–439, Philadelphia, June 1990.

[BK85]   J. A. Bergstra and J. W. Klop. Algebra of communicating processes with abstraction. *Theoretical Computer Science*, 37(1):77–121, 1985.

[Bry92]   R.E. Bryant. Symbolic boolean manipulation with ordered binary-decision diagrams. *ACM Computing Surveys*, 24(3):293–318, 1992.

[Büc62]   J.R. Büchi. On a decision method in restricted second order arithmetic. In *Proc. Internat. Congr. Logic, Method and Philos. Sci. 1960*, pages 1–12, Stanford, 1962. Stanford University Press.

[CC77]   P. Cousot and R. Cousot. Abstract interpreatation: A unified lattice model for static analysis of programs by construction or approximation of fixpoints. In *Proceedings of the Fourth Annual ACM Symposium on Principles of Programming Languages*, January 1977.

[CES86]   E.M. Clarke, E.A. Emerson, and A.P. Sistla. Automatic verification of finite-state concurrent systems using temporal logic specifications. *ACM Transactions on Programming Languages and Systems*, 8(2):244–263, January 1986.

[CGL92]   E.M. Clarke, O. Grumberg, and D. E. Long. Model checking and abstraction. In *Proceedings of the 19th Annual ACM Symposium on Principles of Programming Languages*, January 1992.

[CLM89]   E.M. Clarke, D. E. Long, and K.L. McMillan. Compositional model checking. In *Proceedings of the 4th Symposium on Logic in Computer Science*, 1989.

[CM88]   K. M. Chandy and J. Misra. *Parallel Program Design: A Foundation*. Addison-Wesley, 1988.

[DDHY92]   D. L. Dill, A. J. Drexler, A. J. Hu, and C. H. Yang. Protocol verification as a hardware design aid. In *1992 IEEE International Conference on Computer Design: VLSI in Computers and Processors*, pages 522–525, Cambridge, MA, October 1992. IEEE Computer Society.

[Dij76]   E. W. Dijkstra. *A Discipline of Programming*. Prentice-Hall, 1976.

[Dil89]   D. L. Dill. *Trace Theory for Automatic Hierarchical Verification of Speed-Independent Circuits*. ACM Distinguished Dissertations. MIT Press, 1989.

[EF82]   T. Elrad and N. Francez. Decomposition of distributed programs into communication closed layers. *Science of Computer Programming*, 2:155–173, 1982.

[Esp94]   J. Esparza. Model checking using net unfoldings. *Science of Computer Programming*, 23:151–195, 1994.

[FGM+92]   J.C. Fernandez, H. Garavel, L. Mounier, A. Rasse, C. Rodriguez, and J. Sifakis. A toolbox for the verification of LOTOS programs. In *Proc. of the 14th International Conference on Software Engineering ICSE'14*, Melbourne, Australia, May 1992. ACM.

[Fra86]   N. Francez. *Fairness*. Springer-Verlag, 1986.

[GH85] M. G. Gouda and J. Y. Han. Protocol validation by fair progress state exploration. *Computer Networks and ISDN systems*, pages 353–361, May 1985.

[GH93] P. Godefroid and G. J. Holzmann. On the verification of temporal properties. In *Proc. 13th IFIP WG 6.1 International Symposium on Protocol Specification, Testing, and Verification*, pages 109–124, Liège, May 1993. North-Holland.

[GHP92] P. Godefroid, G. J. Holzmann, and D. Pirottin. State space caching revisited. In *Proc. 4th Workshop on Computer Aided Verification*, volume 663 of *Lecture Notes in Computer Science*, pages 178–191, Montreal, June 1992. Springer-Verlag.

[GK91] P. Godefroid and F. Kabanza. An efficient reactive planner for synthesizing reactive plans. In *Proceedings of AAAI-91*, volume 2, pages 640–645, Anaheim, July 1991.

[GKPP94] R. Gerth, R. Kuiper, D. Peled, and W. Penczek. A partial order approach to branching time model checking. Proceedings of the Third Israel Symposium on Theory of Computing and Systems, 1994.

[GL93] S. Graf and C. Loiseaux. A tool for symbolic program verification and abstraction. In *Proc. 5th Conference on Computer Aided Verification*, volume 697 of *Lecture Notes in Computer Science*, pages 71–84, Elounda, June 1993. Springer-Verlag.

[God90] P. Godefroid. Using partial orders to improve automatic verification methods. In *Proc. 2nd Workshop on Computer Aided Verification*, volume 531 of *Lecture Notes in Computer Science*, pages 176–185, Rutgers, June 1990. Springer-Verlag. Extended version in ACM/AMS DIMACS Series, volume 3, pages 321–340, 1991.

[GP93] P. Godefroid and D. Pirottin. Refining dependencies improves partial-order verification methods. In *Proc. 5th Conference on Computer Aided Verification*, volume 697 of *Lecture Notes in Computer Science*, pages 438–449, Elounda, June 1993. Springer-Verlag.

[Gri90] E. P. Gribomont. A programming logic for formal concurrent systems. In *Proc. CONCUR'90*, volume 458 of *Lecture Notes in Computer Science*, pages 298–313. Springer-Verlag, 1990.

[Gri93]   E. P. Gribomont. Concurrency without toil: a systematic method for par-
            allel program design. *Science of Computer Programming*, 21:1–56, 1993.

[GS90]   S. Graf and B. Steffen. Compositional minimization of finite-state systems.
            In *Proc. 2nd Workshop on Computer Aided Verification*, volume 531 of
            Lecture Notes in Computer Science, Rutgers, June 1990. Springer-Verlag.

[GW91a]   P. Godefroid and P. Wolper. A partial approach to model checking. In
            Proceedings of the 6th IEEE Symposium on Logic in Computer Science,
            pages 406–415, Amsterdam, July 1991.

[GW91b]   P. Godefroid and P. Wolper. Using partial orders for the efficient verifica-
            tion of deadlock freedom and safety properties. In *Proc. 3rd Workshop on
            Computer Aided Verification*, volume 575 of *Lecture Notes in Computer
            Science*, pages 332–342, Aalborg, July 1991.

[GW93]   P. Godefroid and P. Wolper. Using partial orders for the efficient ver-
            ification of deadlock freedom and safety properties. *Formal Methods in
            System Design*, 2(2):149–164, April 1993.

[GW94]   P. Godefroid and P. Wolper. A partial approach to model checking. *In-
            formation and Computation*, 110(2):305–326, May 1994.

[HD93]   A. J. Hu and D. L. Dill. Efficient verification with bdds using implicitly
            conjoined invariants. In *Proc. 5th Conference on Computer Aided Veri-
            fication*, volume 697 of *Lecture Notes in Computer Science*, pages 3–14,
            Elounda, June 1993. Springer-Verlag.

[Hen88]   M. Hennessy. *Algebraic Theory of Processes*. MIT Press, 1988.

[HGP92]   G. J. Holzmann, P. Godefroid, and D. Pirottin. Coverage preserving reduc-
            tion strategies for reachability analysis. In *Proc. 12th IFIP WG 6.1 Inter-
            national Symposium on Protocol Specification, Testing, and Verification*,
            pages 349–363, Lake Buena Vista, Florida, June 1992. North-Holland.

[HK90]   Z. Har'El and R. P. Kurshan. Software for analytical development of
            communication protocols. *AT&T Technical Journal*, 1990.

[Hoa85]   C. A. R. Hoare. *Communicating Sequential Processes*. Prentice-Hall, 1985.

[Hol85]   G. J. Holzmann.   Tracing protocols.   *AT&T Technical Journal*,
            64(12):2413–2434, 1985.

[Hol87]   G. J. Holzmann. Automated protocol validation in argos — assertion
           proving and scatter searching. *IEEE Trans. on Software Engineering*,
           13(6):683–696, 1987.

[Hol91]   G. J. Holzmann. *Design and Validation of Computer Protocols*. Prentice
           Hall, 1991.

[HP94]   G. J. Holzmann and D. Peled. An improvement in formal verification. In
           Proc. FORTE'94, pages 177–191, Bern, 1994.

[JJ91]   C. Jard and Th. Jeron. Bounded-memory algorithms for verification on-
           the-fly. In *Proc. 3rd Workshop on Computer Aided Verification*, volume
           575 of *Lecture Notes in Computer Science*, Aalborg, July 1991. Springer-
           Verlag.

[JK90]   R. Janicki and M. Koutny. On some implementation of optimal simula-
           tions. In *Proc. 2nd Workshop on Computer Aided Verification*, volume
           531 of *Lecture Notes in Computer Science*, pages 166–175, Rutgers, June
           1990. Springer-Verlag.

[JZ93]   W. Janssen and J. Zwiers. Specifying and proving communication closed-
           ness in protocols. In *Proc. 13th IFIP WG 6.1 International Symposium
           on Protocol Specification, Testing, and Verification*, pages 323–339, Liège,
           May 1993. North-Holland.

[KM89]   R. P. Kurshan and K. McMillan. A structural induction theorem for
           processes. In *Proceedings of the Eigth ACM Symposium on Principles of
           Distributed Computing*, pages 239–248, Edmonton, Alberta, August 1989.

[KP86]   Y. Kornatzky and S. S. Pinter. A model checker for partial order temporal
           logic. EE PUB 597, Department of Electrical Enginering, Technion-Israel
           Institute of Technology, 1986.

[KP87]   S. Katz and D. Peled. Interleaving set temporal logic. In *Proc. 6th ACM
           Symp. on Principles of Distributed Computing*, pages 178–190, Vancouver,
           August 1987.

[KP92a]   S. Katz and D. Peled. Defining conditional independence using collapses.
           Theoretical Computer Science, 101:337–359, 1992.

[KP92b]   S. Katz and D. Peled. Verification of distributed programs using repre-
           sentative interleaving sequences. *Distributed Computing*, 6:107–120, 1992.

[Kur89]   R. P. Kurshan. Analysis of discrete event coordination. In *Proceedings of the REX Workshop on Stepwise Refinement of Distributed Systems, Models, Formalisms, Correctness*, volume 430 of *Lecture Notes in Computer Science*, May 1989.

[Lam77]   L. Lamport. Proving the correctness of multiprocess programs. *IEEE Transactions on Software Engineering*, SE-3(2):125–143, 1977.

[Lam78]   L. Lamport. Time, clocks, and the ordering of events in a distributed system. *Communications of the ACM*, 21(7):558–564, 1978.

[Lam83]   L. Lamport. What good is temporal logic? *Information Processing'83*, pages 657–668, 1983.

[Liu89]   M.T. Liu. Protocol engineering. *Advances in Computing*, 29:79–195, 1989.

[Lon93]   David Long. *Model Checking, Abstraction, and Compositional Verification*. PhD thesis, Carnegie Mellon University, July 1993.

[LP81]   H. R. Lewis and C. H. Papadimitriou. *Elements of the Theory of Computation*. Prentice Hall, 1981.

[LP85]   O. Lichtenstein and A. Pnueli. Checking that finite state concurrent programs satisfy their linear specification. In *Proceedings of the Twelfth ACM Symposium on Principles of Programming Languages*, pages 97–107, New Orleans, January 1985.

[Maz86]   A. Mazurkiewicz. Trace theory. In *Petri Nets: Applications and Relationships to Other Models of Concurrency, Advances in Petri Nets 1986, Part II; Proceedings of an Advanced Course*, volume 255 of *Lecture Notes in Computer Science*, pages 279–324. Springer-Verlag, 1986.

[McM92]   K. McMillan. Using unfolding to avoid the state explosion problem in the verification of asynchronous circuits. In *Proc. 4th Workshop on Computer Aided Verification*, volume 663 of *Lecture Notes in Computer Science*, pages 164–177, Montreal, June 1992. Springer-Verlag.

[McM93]   K. L. McMillan. *Symbolic Model Checking*. Kluwer Academic Publishers, 1993.

[Mil80]   R. Milner. *A Calculus of Communicating Systems*, volume 92 of *Lecture Notes in Computer Science*. Springer-Verlag, 1980.

[MP92]   Z. Manna and A. Pnueli. *The Temporal Logic of Reactive and Concurrent Systems: Specification.* Springer-Verlag, 1992.

[Ove81]   W. T. Overman. *Verification of Concurrent Systems: Function and Timing.* PhD thesis, University of California Los Angeles, 1981.

[Pel93]   D. Peled. All from one, one for all: on model checking using representatives. In *Proc. 5th Conference on Computer Aided Verification*, volume 697 of *Lecture Notes in Computer Science*, pages 409–423, Elounda, June 1993. Springer-Verlag.

[Pel94]   D. Peled. Combining partial order reductions with on-the-fly model-checking. In *Proc. 6th Conference on Computer Aided Verification*, volume 818 of *Lecture Notes in Computer Science*, pages 377–390, Stanford, June 1994. Springer-Verlag.

[Pen88]   W. Penczek. A temporal logic for event structures. *Fundamenta Informaticae*, 11(3):297–326, 1988.

[Pen90]   W. Penczek. Proving partial order properties using CCTL. Proc. Concurrency and Compositionality Workshop, San Miniato, Italy, 1990.

[Pet81]   J. L. Peterson. *Petri Net Theory and the Modeling of Systems.* Prentice Hall, 1981.

[PL90]   D. K. Probst and H. F. Li. Using partial-order semantics to avoid the state explosion problem in asynchronous systems. In *Proc. 2nd Workshop on Computer Aided Verification*, volume 531 of *Lecture Notes in Computer Science*, pages 146–155, Rutgers, June 1990. Springer-Verlag.

[Pnu85]   A. Pnueli. Applications of temporal logic to the specification and verification of reactive systems: A survey of current trends. In *Proc. Advanced School on Current Trends in Concurrency*, volume 224 of *Lecture Notes in Computer Science*, pages 510–584, Berlin, 1985. Springer-Verlag.

[Pra86]   V. Pratt. Modelling concurrency with partial orders. *International Journal of Parallel Programming*, 15(1):33–71, 1986.

[PW84]   S. S. Pinter and P. Wolper. A temporal logic for reasoning about partially ordered computations. In *Proc. 3rd ACM Symposium on Principles of Distributed Computing*, pages 28–37, Vancouver, 1984.

[QS81]   J.P. Quielle and J. Sifakis. Specification and verification of concurrent
           systems in CESAR. In *Proc. 5th Int'l Symp. on Programming*, volume 137
           of *Lecture Notes in Computer Science*, pages 337–351. Springer-Verlag,
           1981.

[Rei85]   W. Reisig. *Petri Nets: an Introduction*. EATCS Monographs on Theoret-
           ical Computer Science, Springer-Verlag, 1985.

[Rud87]   H. Rudin. Network protocols and tools to help produce them. *Annual
           Review of Computer Science*, 2:291–316, 1987.

[Rud92]   H. Rudin. Protocol development success stories: Part I. In *Proc. 12th IFIP
           WG 6.1 International Symposium on Protocol Specification, Testing, and
           Verification*, Lake Buena Vista, Florida, June 1992. North-Holland.

[SdR89]   F. A. Stomp and W. P. de Roever. Designing distributed algorithms by
           means of formal sequentially phased reasoning. In *Proc. 3rd Interna-
           tional Workshop on Distributed Algorithms*, volume 392 of *Lecture Notes
           in Computer Science*, pages 242–253, Nice, 1989. Springer-Verlag.

[Sif82]   J. Sifakis. A unified approach for studying the properties of transition
           system. *Theoretical Computer Science*, 18:227–258, 1982.

[Tar72]   R. E. Tarjan. Depth-first search and linear graph algorithms. *SIAM J.
           Computing*, 1(2):146–160, 1972.

[Tha89]   André Thayse and et al. *From Modal Logic to Deductive Databases: In-
           troducing a Logic Based Approach to Artificial Intelligence*. Wiley, 1989.

[TN87]   M. Trehel and M. Naimi. Un algorithme distribué d'exclusion mutuelle
           en log(n). *Technique et Science Informatiques*, pages 141–150, 1987.

[Tur93]   K. J. Turner et al. *Using Formal Description Techniques – An Introduction
           to Estelle, Lotos and SDL*. Wiley, 1993.

[Val88a]   A. Valmari. Error detection by reduced reachability graph generation. In
           *Proc. 9th International Conference on Application and Theory of Petri
           Nets*, pages 95–112, Venice, 1988.

[Val88b]   A. Valmari. Heuristics for lazy state generation speeds up analysis of con-
           current systems. In *Proc. of the Finnish Artificial Intelligence Symposium
           STeP-88*, volume 2, pages 640–650, Helsinki, 1988.

[Val90]   A. Valmari. A stubborn attack on state explosion. In *Proc. 2nd Workshop on Computer Aided Verification*, volume 531 of *Lecture Notes in Computer Science*, pages 156–165, Rutgers, June 1990. Springer-Verlag.

[Val91]   A. Valmari. Stubborn sets for reduced state space generation. In *Advances in Petri Nets 1990*, volume 483 of *Lecture Notes in Computer Science*, pages 491–515. Springer-Verlag, 1991.

[Val93]   A. Valmari. On-the-fly verification with stubborn sets. In *Proc. 5th Conference on Computer Aided Verification*, volume 697 of *Lecture Notes in Computer Science*, pages 397–408, Elounda, June 1993. Springer-Verlag.

[VW86]   M.Y. Vardi and P. Wolper. An automata-theoretic approach to automatic program verification. In *Proceedings of the First Symposium on Logic in Computer Science*, pages 322–331, Cambridge, June 1986.

[Wes86]   C. H. West. Protocol validation by random state exploration. In *Proc. 6th IFIP WG 6.1 International Symposium on Protocol Specification, Testing, and Verification*, pages 233–242. North-Holland, 1986.

[WG93]   P. Wolper and P. Godefroid. Partial-order methods for temporal verification (invited paper). In *Proc. CONCUR'93*, volume 715 of *Lecture Notes in Computer Science*, pages 233–246, Hildesheim, August 1993. Springer-Verlag.

[Win86]   G. Winskel. Event structures. In *Petri Nets: Applications and Relationships to Other Models of Concurrency, Advances in Petri Nets 1986, Part II; Proceedings of an Advanced Course*, volume 255 of *Lecture Notes in Computer Science*, pages 325–392. Springer-Verlag, 1986.

[WL89]   P. Wolper and V. Lovinfosse. Verifying properties of large sets of processes with network invariants. In *Automatic Verification Methods for Finite State Systems, Proc. Int. Workshop, Grenoble*, volume 407 of *Lecture Notes in Computer Science*, pages 68–80, Grenoble, June 1989. Springer-Verlag.

[Wol89]   P. Wolper. On the relation of programs and computations to models of temporal logic. In B. Banieqbal, H. Barringer, and A. Pnueli, editors, *Proc. Temporal Logic in Specification*, volume 398 of *Lecture Notes in Computer Science*, pages 75–123. Springer-Verlag, 1989.

[WVS83]   P. Wolper, M.Y. Vardi, and A.P. Sistla. Reasoning about infinite compu-
          tation paths. In *Proc. 24th IEEE Symposium on Foundations of Computer
          Science*, pages 185–194, Tucson, 1983.

[YSSC93] T. Yoneda, A. Shibayama, B.-H. Schlingloff, and E. Clarke. Efficient verifi-
          cation of parallel real-time systems. In *Proc. 5th Conference on Computer
          Aided Verification*, volume 697 of *Lecture Notes in Computer Science*,
          pages 321–332, Elounda, June 1993. Springer-Verlag.

Index

Springer-Verlag
and the Environment

We at Springer-Verlag firmly believe that an international science publisher has a special obligation to the environment, and our corporate policies consistently reflect this conviction.

We also expect our business partners – paper mills, printers, packaging manufacturers, etc. – to commit themselves to using environmentally friendly materials and production processes.

The paper in this book is made from low- or no-chlorine pulp and is acid free, in conformance with international standards for paper permanency.

Lecture Notes in Computer Science

For information about Vols. 1–957

please contact your bookseller or Springer-Verlag